EARTH CARE

Forestry & Farming

SUNNYSIDE PRIMARY SCHOOL

Miles Litvinoff

Heinemann

Editor
Judy Garlick

Designer
Malcolm Smythe

Managing editor
Lionel Bender

Art editor
Ben White

FORESTRY AND FARMING (Earthcare)
was produced for Gaia Books by
Bender Richardson White, Uxbridge, UK.
This edition first published in Great Britain in 1997
by Heinemann Library
Halley Court, Jordan Hill, Oxford OX2 8EJ
a division of Reed Educational & Professional
Publishing Ltd
Oxford Florence Prague Madrid Athens
Melbourne Auckland Kuala Lumpur Singapore Tokyo
Ibadan Nairobi Kampala Johannesburg Gaborone
Portsmouth NH (USA) Chicago Mexico City São Paulo

Gaia Books Limited
66 Charlotte Street, London W1P 1LR and
20 High Street, Stroud GL5 1AS

Reproduction MRM Graphics, Winslow, Bucks, England

Printed in Spain

00 99 98 97 96
10 9 8 7 6 5 4 3 2 1

ISBN 0 431 07729 0
This title is also available in a hardback library edition
ISBN 0 431 07728 2

British Library Cataloguing in Publication Data
Litvinoff, Miles
Forestry and Farming. – (Earthcare)
1. Forests and forestry – Juvenile literature 2. Agriculture
– Juvenile literature
I. Title
630

Acknowledgements
Production: Kim Richardson, Susan Walby
Direction: Patrick Nugent, Pip Morgan, Joss Pearson;
Publisher Liason Hannah Wheeler, at Gaia Books.

Illustrations David Ashby; Norman Barber (Linden
Artists); Martin Camm (Linden Artists); Jim Channel
(Linden Artists); Stefan Chabluk; David Cook; Bill Donohoe;
Eugene Fleury; Chris Forsey; Aziz Khan; David Mallot; Gary
Marsh; Francesca Pelizzoli; John Potter; David Salariya;
Ann Savage; John Shipperbottom; Rob Shone; Nicky Snell
(Virgil Pomfret Agency); Clive Spong (Linden Artists);
Roger Stewart (Virgil Pomfret Agency); Alan Suttie; George
Thompson; Shirley Willis.

Photographs The publishers would like to thank the
following for permission to reproduce photographs: pages
4–5 Holt Studios International/Silvestre Silva. 10 Overseas
Devlopment Administration, London. 12–13 Hilary
Coulby/Oxfam. 16 Sarah Errington/Oxfam. 19 Jeremy
Hartley/Oxfam. 21 Rob Cousins/Oxfam. 23 Jeremy
Hartley/Oxfam. 24–25 (main) Sean Sprague/Oxfam; (rest)
Keith Bernstein/Oxfam. 26 Environmental Picture
Library/Jeff Libman. 28–29 Holt Studios International/Inga
Spence. 32 Penny Tweedie/Oxfam. 37 Sean Sprague/
Oxfam. 38–39 (all) Geoff Sayer/Oxfam. 43 Geoff Sayer/
Oxfam.
Cover photographs Image Bank
Cover design Simon Balley Design Associates

*The publishers would like to thank Koos Neefjes, Amanda
Barker, and Fred Martin for their helpful comments on the
text. Bender Richardson White would like thank John
Stidworthy for help in planning the book, and Liz Clayton
and Anna Coryndon at Oxfam for producing the Gaiawatch
articles and supplying photographs.*

MILES LITVINOFF is a specialist writer and editor of books on
environment, development, and human rights for children
and adults. He works as an editor for the Minority Rights
Group, a human rights organization in London, and tutors
the Open University Environment course. He is author and
editor of many successful titles, including *The Greening of
Aid: Sustainable Livelihoods in Practice* (co-editor, 1988),
The Earthscan Action Handbook for People and Planet
(1990), *Ancestors: The Origins of the People and Countries
of Europe* (co-author, 1992), the *Junior Cultural Atlas* series
(1989–94), and *The World Minorities Directory* (1996).

CONTENTS

ABOUT THIS BOOK

This book is part of a four-title series that explains our place on the Earth, the environmental problems we face, the kind of solutions we need, and how people are already working to put good ideas into practice.

Underlying the approach in the books is the Gaia theory, named after the Earth goddess of ancient Greece. The space scientist James Lovelock first proposed the Gaia theory in the 1970s. The theory suggests that the biosphere – the thin layer between the Earth's rocky surface and outer space, the home of plants and animals, including ourselves – is a living organism. Life has created and maintained the conditions it needs for its own survival. The Earth does not need the human species, but we may not survive unless we safeguard the natural resources on which we depend.

Another important idea is justice, or fairness. The brutal poverty experienced by one person in every four involves the denial of many basic and interconnected human rights. Poverty on this huge scale is largely, although not only, the result of human choices and actions. Better decisions by individuals, small groups, larger communities, countries, and governments can therefore make the world a fairer place.

Many of the most urgent environmental problems result from extremes of wealth and poverty. The very rich cause immense environmental damage by consuming too much, while the poor degrade their surroundings in the struggle to survive. Working to safeguard our environment and working for a fairer world are closely connected.

Forestry and Farming begins with an introductory chapter describing the formation and "life story" of our planet, as well as the natural processes on which living things depend. It summarizes the changes that human development has produced in the natural environment and considers why many people are concerned about our future. This is followed by a description of the environmental challenges we face in connection with our use of soil and the way we produce, distribute, and consume food. The first chapter, **Land and Trees,** describes plant and tree growth, soil damage and deforestation, and how we can protect land and forests. The second chapter, **Food and Farming,** focuses on crops and livestock, traditional and modern agriculture, food distribution, world hunger, and the future of farming.

Each chapter contains information and ideas laid out in self-contained two-page sections, or "spreads" Each spread combines text, maps, diagrams, and photographs, and takes one of three viewpoints: Resources, Problems, or Solutions. Both chapters also include an illustrated "Gaia Watch" case study, provided by Oxfam, and two further features: "Do you know?" boxes provide additional facts, figures, and examples not contained in the main text; while "Home action" boxes suggest what we can do within our community to tackle problems.

At the end of the book, before the index, there is a world political map, accompanied by facts and figures about continents, regions, and countries, and a glossary of terms. We explain new, difficult, and important terms the first time they are used in the text: these terms are in **bold** if they appear in the glossary. Some terms, however, need a brief mention here.

We often describe countries as either "developed" or "developing" (although the terms do not fit all countries equally well). Developed countries are those where large-scale industry, based on burning coal, oil, and gas, is well established and usually the main source of jobs and wealth creation. These countries control most international trade and are generally rich. Developing countries are those where farming is still the main way of life. Most developing countries are poor. There are many more developing than developed countries. We also use the terms "North" and "South", broadly to mean the same as "developed", or "rich", and "developing", or "poor". All industrialized countries, apart from Australia and New Zealand, are in the northern hemisphere, while most developing countries are in the southern hemisphere.

We use the US dollar as the standard measure of money, which is common for international comparisons. As a rough guide, you can convert dollars to pounds sterling on the basis of $1.50 = £1.

Abbreviations
The following abbreviations are used in the series:

%: per cent	m²: square metre	g: gram
cm: centimetre	ha: hectare	kg: kilogram
m: metre	m³: cubic metre	t: tonne
km: kilometre	km³: cubic kilometre	kW: kilowatt
		kWh: kilowatt-hour

INTRODUCTION

"At first I thought I was fighting to save rubber trees. Then I thought I was fighting to save the Amazon rainforest. Now I realize I am fighting for humanity."
FRANCISCO CHICO MENDES,
Brazilian rubber tappers' leader,
shot dead in 1988

The Earth is a remarkable planet. Its old age and ancient beginnings, the fact that life exists at all, and the huge variety of life forms: all are part of an amazing story. Humanity has become part of this story. At first we were just one kind of animal among many. With time, we came to consider ourselves something apart from the rest of nature. We behave as though we have conquered nature and forget we are a part of it. Much of this so-called "conquest" has produced bad results: polluted skies and waters, land stripped bare of trees, dwindling animal populations, and millions of people living in poverty. We need to learn from our mistakes, acquire a greater sense of responsibility towards our surroundings and our fellow human beings, and begin to repair the damage.

The world's tropical rainforests lie close to the equator where hot, wet conditions encourage dense plant growth. This aerial photograph shows the rainforest canopy, which hides a wealth of plant and animal species below. The world's rainforests are among the regions most at risk from human activities.

SPACESHIP EARTH

Space travel, though exciting, involves risk and danger. Astronauts must operate their equipment carefully, because mistakes can be fatal. Our planet is sometimes compared with a spacecraft, travelling with the rest of the Solar System through space. We need to understand how our "craft" works, and respect it.

DO YOU KNOW?

The biosphere and Gaia

Living things inhabit the Earth from the deepest sea to the highest mountain peak and the air above it. Yet, compared with the size of the planet, this layer of life is as thin as the surface dew on the skin of an apple. We call this living layer the **biosphere** (from the Greek *bios*, meaning life).

Plants, animals, and the environment they share depend on and affect each other. Even the ocean floor is constantly being created. The interrelated nature of all things on Earth means that the planet itself resembles a single, giant, living **organism**. The scientist James Lovelock coined the term Gaia (the name of the ancient Greek goddess of the Earth) to describe our world and all the life it contains.

Orbiting the Sun, our world seems small and alone. The way it supports its living "passengers" appears unique. Astronomers have not yet detected any other planet in the universe showing signs of life.

The Earth formed from gases and dust 4500 million years ago. The planet's centre is white hot; at the upper edge of the Earth's **atmosphere**, the air is too cold and thin for our survival. Life began to **evolve** between these hot and cold extremes 3700 million years ago. The mix of gases in the air, and the Earth's surface temperature, probably changed when life began.

Global interaction

Plants and animals, humans included, have developed together and affect each other in more ways than we fully know. Living things also interact with the **environment** (our surroundings). From the tiniest soil **microbe** to the mightiest whale, we all depend on the flow of energy from the Sun.

Plants convert solar energy into forms that animals can use to breathe and eat. Water, oxygen, and **carbon dioxide** also flow through the "life systems". These flows take place during breathing, photosynthesis (the manufacture of **carbohydrates** by plants, using sunlight), feeding, and the decay of dead matter.

The Earth has survived major changes to its air, land and sea, **climate**, and life forms over millions of years. Many species have evolved, and many have died out. A vast range of human activities have similarly, but much more recently, had a great impact on the planet.

THE LIFE-SUPPORTING PLANET
A layer of gases – the atmosphere – helps warm the Earth and shields living things from the Sun's harmful **ultraviolet (UV)** rays. Surfaces that reflect sunlight, such as ice, prevent overheating of the biosphere. Plants use energy from sunlight, carbon dioxide and oxygen, and water to make food. Animals get their food from plants, and oxygen from the air or water. Warm water rises from the sea as vapour, forming clouds which eventually water the land.

The Earth's atmosphere before life began was probably similar to that of Venus or Mars. The planet's surface was very hot. Early life forms helped change the gas mixture by absorbing carbon dioxide (CO_2) and releasing oxygen (O_2). (N is the symbol for nitrogen.)

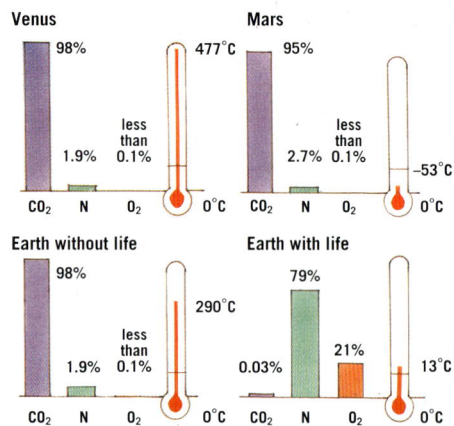

Venus — CO_2 98%, N 1.9%, O_2 less than 0.1%, 477°C

Mars — CO_2 95%, N 2.7%, O_2 less than 0.1%, −53°C

Earth without life — CO_2 98%, N 1.9%, O_2 less than 0.1%, 290°C

Earth with life — CO_2 0.03%, N 79%, O_2 21%, 13°C

Life on Earth depends on many complicated, interacting natural processes. For example, warm water rises from the sea as vapour, forming clouds that contribute to the natural "greenhouse effect", which warms the Earth. But the same clouds also reflect the incoming rays of the Sun back into space, cooling the planet. We do not fully understand how these processes affect each other.

Venus

Mars

Natural greenhouse effect warms Earth

Ozone layer shields Earth from Sun's harmful rays

Sunlight reflects from polar ice and other shiny surfaces

Oxygen

Nitrogen

Carbon dioxide

Earth before life began?

Stratosphere, 15–55 km

Lower atmosphere, up to 15 km

Plants grow by absorbing sunlight energy

Nitrogen

Carbon

Animals feed on plants

Nitrogen

Clouds

Carbon dioxide

Water rises into air from sea

Temperature 100 km underground: 3000°C

Water flows back to sea in rivers

Water falls on land as rain, hail, sleet, or snow

OUR CHANGING PLANET

Imagine lilies growing on a pond. If they double in area every day, and take 30 days to cover the whole pond, when will they cover half the pond? Answer: the 29th day. This riddle shows what accelerating change is like: slow at first but frighteningly fast later on. Human beings have changed the face of Earth in much the same way.

The universe has existed since the **Big Bang** simultaneously created space, time, and energy about 15,000 million years ago. Another 10,500 million years passed before the Earth formed. The **evolution** of life began more recently still, first in the oceans and then on land.

Life has evolved over several thousand million years, creating a vast range of **species**. Over time, many new life forms emerged that were more complicated than earlier ones. The most complicated species of all, the highly intelligent human being, is a recent arrival.

From the beginning of time, each new development in the history of the universe and, later, the Earth has happened faster than the previous one. Imagine the whole time span of the universe so far taking place during a 24-hour day. The Big Bang happens in a split-second at 12 midnight. Atoms, the infinitely tiny building blocks of all objects in the universe, come into existence after a few seconds. By 4.00 am the first stars are forming.

Our own Solar System, including planet Earth, begins to take shape only in the late afternoon, at about 5.00 pm.

Life begins in the sea in the early evening, at 6.20 pm. The first land plants and animals appear only at 11.15 at night. The age of dinosaurs lasts from 11.40 pm till six minutes to midnight. The first humans walk upright 10 seconds before midnight. The modern industrial age, which brings huge changes to the planet, lasts for just one-thousandth of a second right at the end of the day.

OUR PLANET'S LIFE STORY
The five globes show the story of life on Earth. The spiral lines represent "time" winding down from past to present. The first globe (far left) illustrates the complete history of our planet – 4500 million years. Because the pace of change has speeded up over time, each of the other globes, from left to right, traces a period 100 times shorter than the previous one. The fifth globe (far right) shows only the last 45 years, a tiny one-hundred-millionth of the Earth's total life span.

4,500 million years

45 million years

450,000 years

4,500 years

45 years

The human impact

We believe that we are the most intelligent species on the planet. We can learn from our mistakes, make decisions affecting our fellow human beings, and plan for the future. We have changed our environment as our activities have become more complex.

Early humans made little difference to their environment. Feeding on plants and animals, they benefited from the way plants convert sunlight into food energy. Later – just 50,000 years ago – they learned to make fire, using

the energy stored in wood. Only in the last 300 years have people burned coal, and later oil and gas.

Like our use of energy, human numbers have grown faster and faster. We have learned how to produce more and more food, control disease, and prolong life. Since the 1830s the population of the world has grown from 1000 million to 5750 million today.

The impact we have had on our surroundings has grown with time,

and the speed of change has built up. More and more problems result from the growing use of coal, oil, and gas, the **overfarming** of soils and **overfishing** of seas, the clearing of forests, and the mining of underground **minerals**.

Unchecked, our growing impact will surely bring about disaster for us. Luckily, there are plenty of practical ideas available for slowing the pace of change and reversing the damage.

THE PACE OF CHANGE
Each graph shows how change has accelerated over time, as human beings have had more and more impact on their surroundings. For hundreds of years the number of people on the planet grew very slowly; the use of energy (animal and water power) changed little; few books and journals existed worldwide; and journeys from place to place were slow. In each of these area there has been a steady increase in the rate of change in the last 300 years, and especially since 1900.

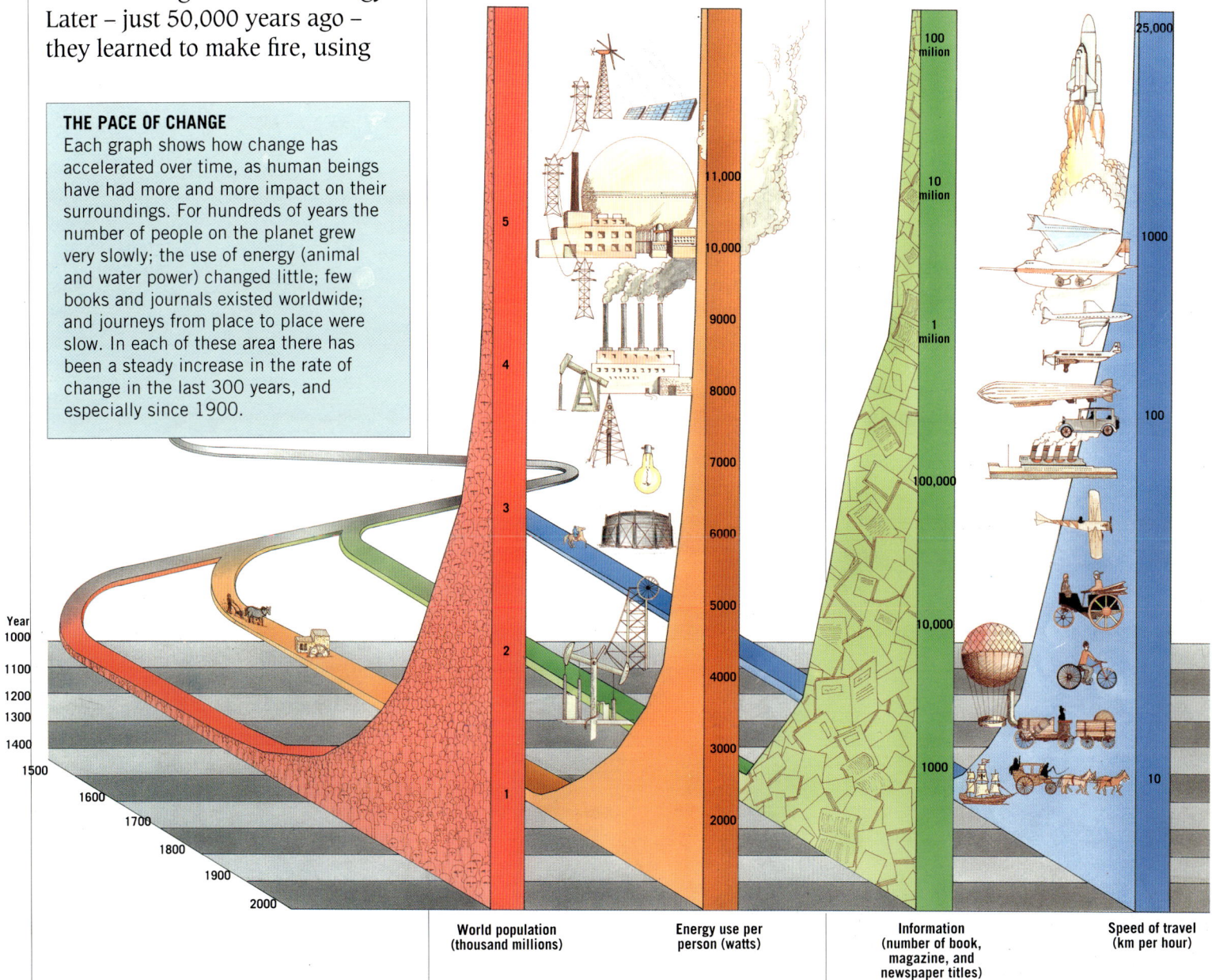

World population (thousand millions)

Energy use per person (watts)

Information (number of book, magazine, and newspaper titles)

Speed of travel (km per hour)

CHALLENGE AHEAD

One person out of every four alive today lives in poverty so severe that they cannot enjoy their basic human rights. And one person in every five uses more resources than is good for the environment. True or false? If you agree that these statements sound true, you are ready to face the challenge ahead.

Modern society consumes vast amounts of the Earth's resources. Yet hundreds of millions of people are poor, hungry, sick, homeless, uneducated, and unemployed. Compared to the rest of the world's population, the richest 1100 million people, mainly in the **developed countries** of the **North**, live lives of luxury.

The wealthiest fifth of humanity causes much of the damage that our planet suffers. They overfarm the best land until soil washes and blows away in rain and wind. They destroy ancient forests in order to grow luxury foods; mine metals to make throw-away drinks cans; sweep the oceans for fish; guzzle oil in cars; and pollute the skies.

This way of life damages the human community as well as the environment. More and more people live in poverty – in both the developed and the **developing** world. More and more conflicts take place about land and limited **resources**. Sometimes these disputes lead to war. Facing all of us is the challenge to try to bring such problems under control. It will not be easy.

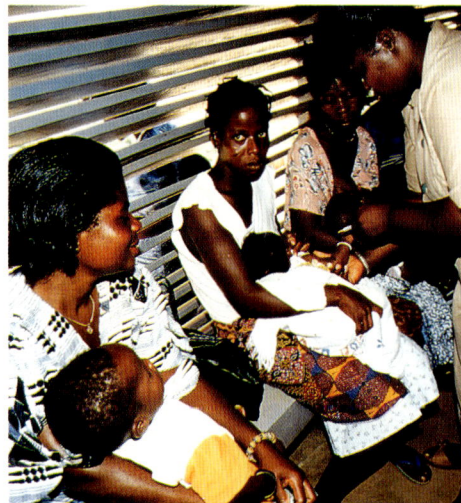

► *This mother-and-baby clinic in Prampram, Ghana, was funded by the British Overseas Development Administration (ODA), an example of the developed world providing practical help for developing countries.*

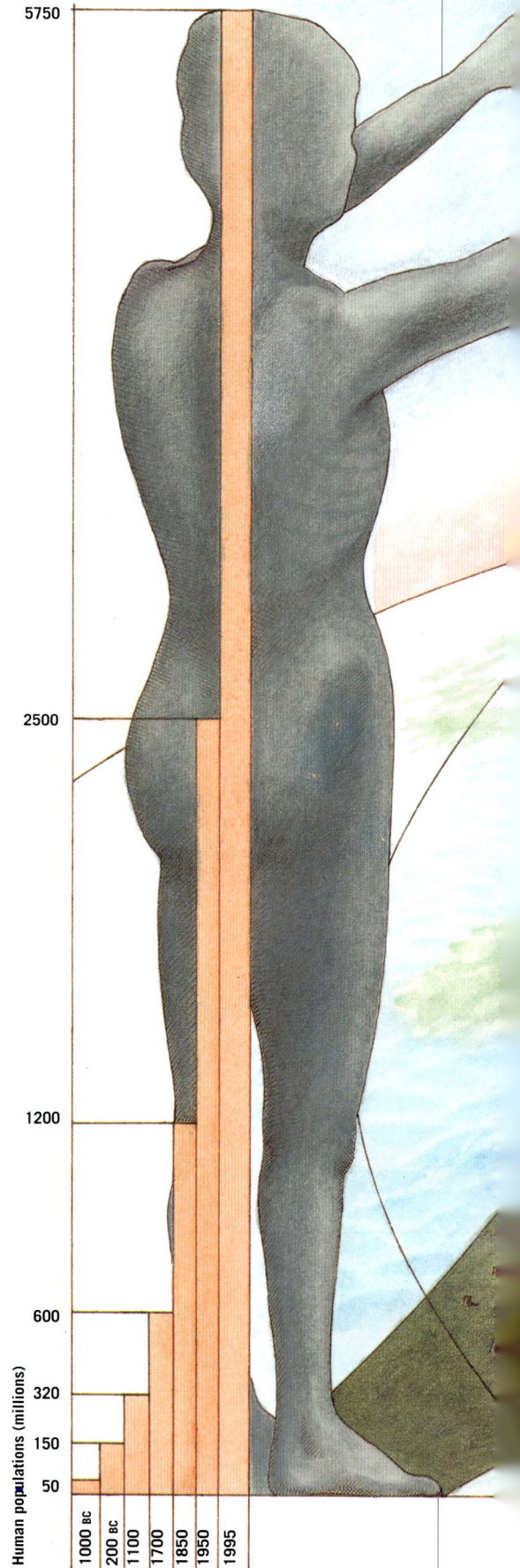

Human populations (millions)

5750

2500

1200

600

320

150

50

1000 BC
200 BC
1100
1700
1850
1950
1995

Early humans caused **deforestation** when they began to clear woodland to create fields. Badly managed farming by early civilizations turned fertile soils in the Middle East and North Africa into desert. Human suffering increased as stronger peoples conquered and ruled over weaker ones. **Pollution** began to affect rivers, coastal waters, and people living in cities.

In the 18th and 19th centuries we began to damage our surroundings even more during the **Industrial Revolution**. Belching chimneys, gushing sewage pipes, and other forms of waste disposal have polluted air, rivers, seas, and land ever since. Key resources such as timber and gas are going up in smoke at an alarming rate. The climate may be changing as a result of air pollution.

Many environmental problems seem to be near to crisis point. The evolution of life itself is under threat as we wipe out natural habitats and species. Where is the pattern of destruction leading us?

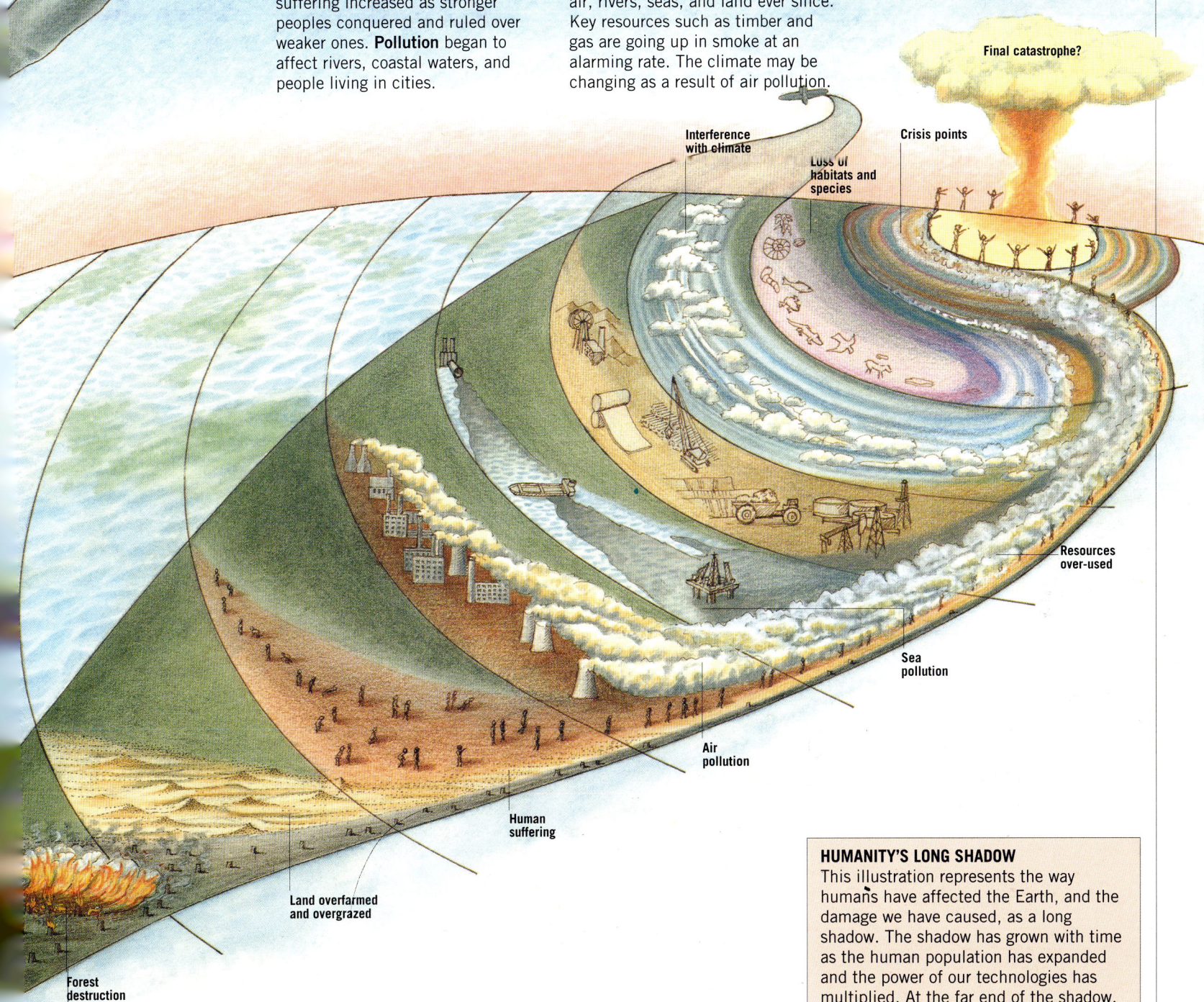

Final catastrophe?

Interference with climate

Loss of habitats and species

Crisis points

Resources over-used

Sea pollution

Air pollution

Human suffering

Land overfarmed and overgrazed

Forest destruction

HUMANITY'S LONG SHADOW
This illustration represents the way humans have affected the Earth, and the damage we have caused, as a long shadow. The shadow has grown with time as the human population has expanded and the power of our technologies has multiplied. At the far end of the shadow, disaster seems to wait for us, perhaps in the form of nuclear war. Surely we can change our ways in time to avoid catastrophe.

LAND

We have no home other than the land. Its plants, animals, and fresh water maintain the air we breathe and provide our food and drink. The fuel and power we use for cooking and heating come directly from trees, or indirectly from the buried, fossilized remains of long-dead creatures and plants, in the form of coal, gas, and oil. Or we harness the power of the Sun, wind, rivers, and waves, using machines that we build from minerals taken from the ground. We also make our buildings, clothes, and possessions from materials on or below the land surface. In the end, everything we have and everything we need depends, in some way, on the land.

Terraces in Banaue, in northern Luzon in the Philippines, enable rice farmers to make intensive use of steep hillsides.

FERTILE SOIL

Next time you are out in the garden, in a park, or in the countryside, think about what is under your feet. Just boring old "earth", "dirt", or "mud"? Maybe. But this thin layer on the planet's surface is essential to all living things. Without the soil, there would be no plants or animals on the land. We had better learn how best to look after it.

LAND AND SOIL TYPES

Every **continent** has different types of soil. Some are well suited to growing crops, but many are not. The diagram shows the world divided into eight land "slices" (continents or regions), the size of each slice reflecting the relative size of that region. It shows six main types of soil and how much of each there is in each region. Of the six soil types, only one is **fertile** (suitable for growing crops). The **percentages** show how much of each soil type there is on Earth (excluding Antarctica and Greenland).

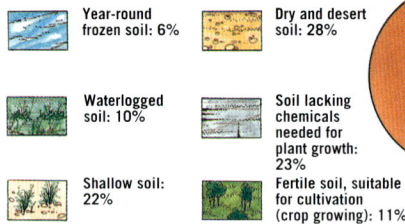

Year-round frozen soil: 6%

Dry and desert soil: 28%

Waterlogged soil: 10%

Soil lacking chemicals needed for plant growth: 23%

Shallow soil: 22%

Fertile soil, suitable for cultivation (crop growing): 11%

The pie chart for each continent or region shows how much of the land people use for crops and grazing animals, and how much is forest. It also shows the percentage of other kinds of land, such as waste land, wild land, built-up areas, and roads.

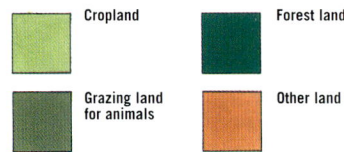

Cropland

Forest land

Grazing land for animals

Other land

▶ **In North and Central America** more than a fifth of the land is suitable for crops, but less than half of the fertile land is farmed. Buildings and roads cover much good soil in the USA.

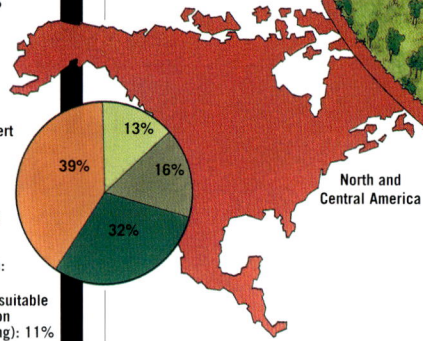

North and Central America

13%
39%
16%
32%

South America

▲ **South America** has large areas of soil lacking many of the chemicals needed by plants, especially in the forest regions. Farmers use less than half the area of fertile soil for growing crops.

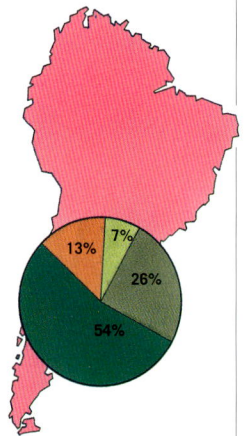

7%
13%
26%
54%

There is a lot more life in a handful of soil than at first meets the eye. At its best, soil is as full of activity and as fascinating as a **rainforest** or a **coral reef**. One **hectare** (ha) of soil (an area about the size of a soccer pitch) may contain up to 300 million mini-beasts such as earthworms, mites, and millipedes. It also contains a vast number of tiny bacteria, algae, and fungi – which are commonly known as microbes. All these living things help to convert complex chemicals

What is soil?

Soil is the uppermost layer of the land surface. It is made up of tiny grains of rock, water, and air. It also contains the remains of dead plants and animals – known as litter before rotting and humus after rotting. Humus is one of the most important ingredients of a fertile soil. Soil is essential for plant growth, providing many chemicals that plants need. The topsoil, nearest the surface, is rich in humus; lower down is the mineral-rich subsoil. Below this is the underlying rock. Roots grow between soil particles to get water, air, and chemicals.

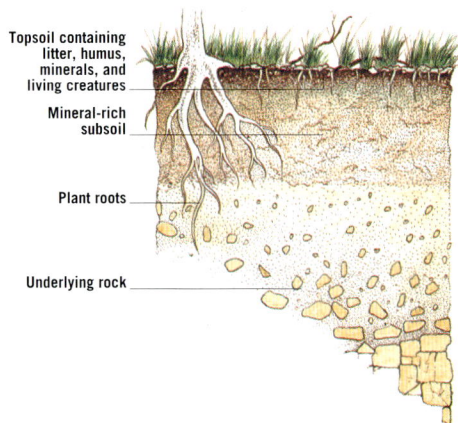

Topsoil containing litter, humus, minerals, and living creatures

Mineral-rich subsoil

Plant roots

Underlying rock

6%
18%
21%
55%

Australasia

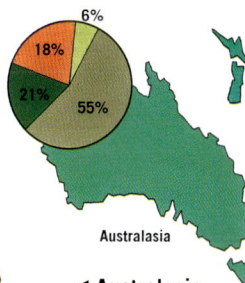

◄ **Australasia** has, for its size, the world's biggest share of dry and desert soil, covering more than half its area. As in **Africa**, farmers cultivate much less land than they could.

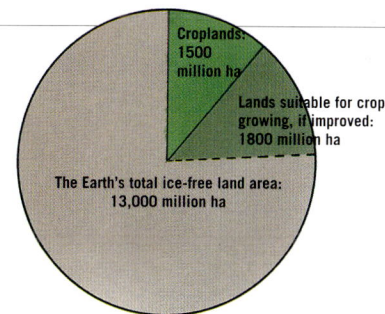

Croplands: 1500 million ha

Lands suitable for crop growing, if improved: 1800 million ha

The Earth's total ice-free land area: 13,000 million ha

How much land do we cultivate?
People grow crops on just over a tenth of the ice-free land surface. With hard work, money, and the right tools we could perhaps double this area.

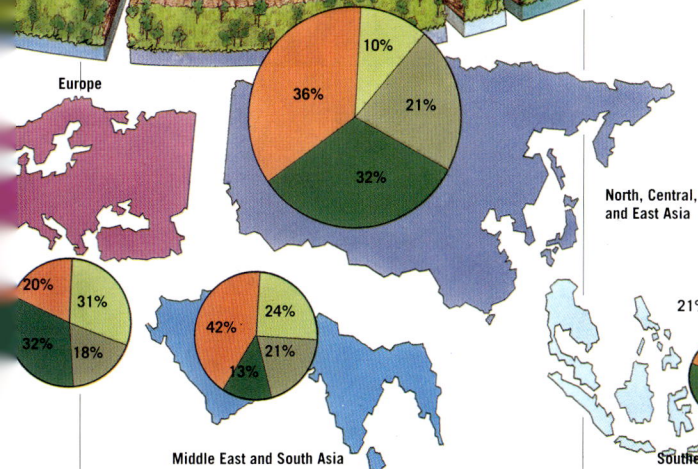

10%
36%
21%
32%

Europe

Africa
6%
26%
44%
24%

North, Central, and East Asia

◄ **Much of Africa** suffers badly from a lack of rainfall, which makes almost half the land too dry for crops. But African farmers use only about a third of the area that is suitable for cultivation.

◄ **North, Central, and East Asia** make up a huge region, but much of the soil is unsuitable for cultivation. More than half the area is too cold or has very thin topsoil. Only a tenth of the land is good for growing crops.

20%
31%
32%
18%

42%
24%
13%
21%

Middle East and South Asia

21% 17% 5%
57%

Southeast Asia

◄ **Southeast Asia** has large areas of poor-quality tropical forest soil. Crops cover almost a fifth of the land, not all of which is naturally suited to farming.

▲ **In Europe**, more than a third of the land is suitable for cultivation. Crops are grown on almost all this land. Compared to its small size as a continent, Europe has the world's largest area of fertile soil.

▲ **The Middle East and South Asia** have large areas of dry land or desert and thin soil. Less than a fifth of the land is suitable for crops; but people use irrigation water to farm almost a quarter of the land.

in soil into forms that plants can take in to help them grow.

Soil varies in quality from region to region, even field to field. To be suitable for growing crops, all the **nutrients** (ingredients necessary for plants to thrive) must be present and in the right amounts. In some regions the soil has too much water and not enough air (as in **wetlands**) or too little water (as in desert) to be fertile. Other soils lack sufficient **humus**, **topsoil**, or living creatures.

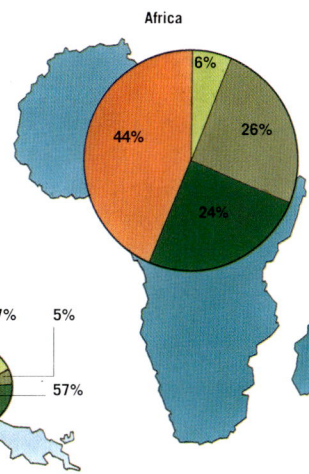

In tropical forests nutrients do not stay in the soil but are quickly taken up by the lush vegetation. In places where people have used modern farming methods over a long period, the soil may contain too few microbes, or have lost important minerals after intensive use, or have been spoilt by too many human-made chemicals. In cold regions the soil may be frozen solid – known as **permafrost** – or be too shallow to allow plants to put down roots.

Soil loss and soil gain
Living and dead plants, animals, and microbes make up only a tiny fraction of soil's weight. Most of the soil consists of small grains of rock, which rainwater, wind, ice, gases in the air, and plant roots have broken down from larger rocks. When a river washes away material, it can deposit a sediment 30 cm deep downstream over 50 years. But when new soil forms by the erosion (wearing away) of rock, it can take 1000 years to create just 1 cm of soil. So 10 cm of soil could take 10,000 years to form – almost as long as recorded human history.

15

PLANT LIFE

Plants are very important to humans. They feed us, clothe us, and help make the air fit to breathe. Plants also help provide water to drink, materials for building and making things, and medicines to take when we are ill. Without plants, we could not live. But plants are not evenly distributed either on the land or in the sea.

Without the Earth's covering of **vegetation** (plants), there would be no animal life. Millions of years ago, the first plants began to change the gases around the Earth – the atmosphere – by increasing the amount of oxygen. All animals need to breathe oxygen to live.

Plants use the energy of sunlight to build up their own supplies of chemical energy, which in turn provide animals with food. All animals either eat plants or feed on other animals that do.

Plants protect the soil from **erosion** by wind or rain, and from drying up in the sun. Their roots take up water from the ground and their leaves let it **evaporate** into the air. This calms or moderates local weather slightly – so conditions are not too dry or too hot – keeping it pleasant for animals and for people. Plants also give us useful materials, ranging from wood and straw for building, to textiles for clothing, and dyes and medicines.

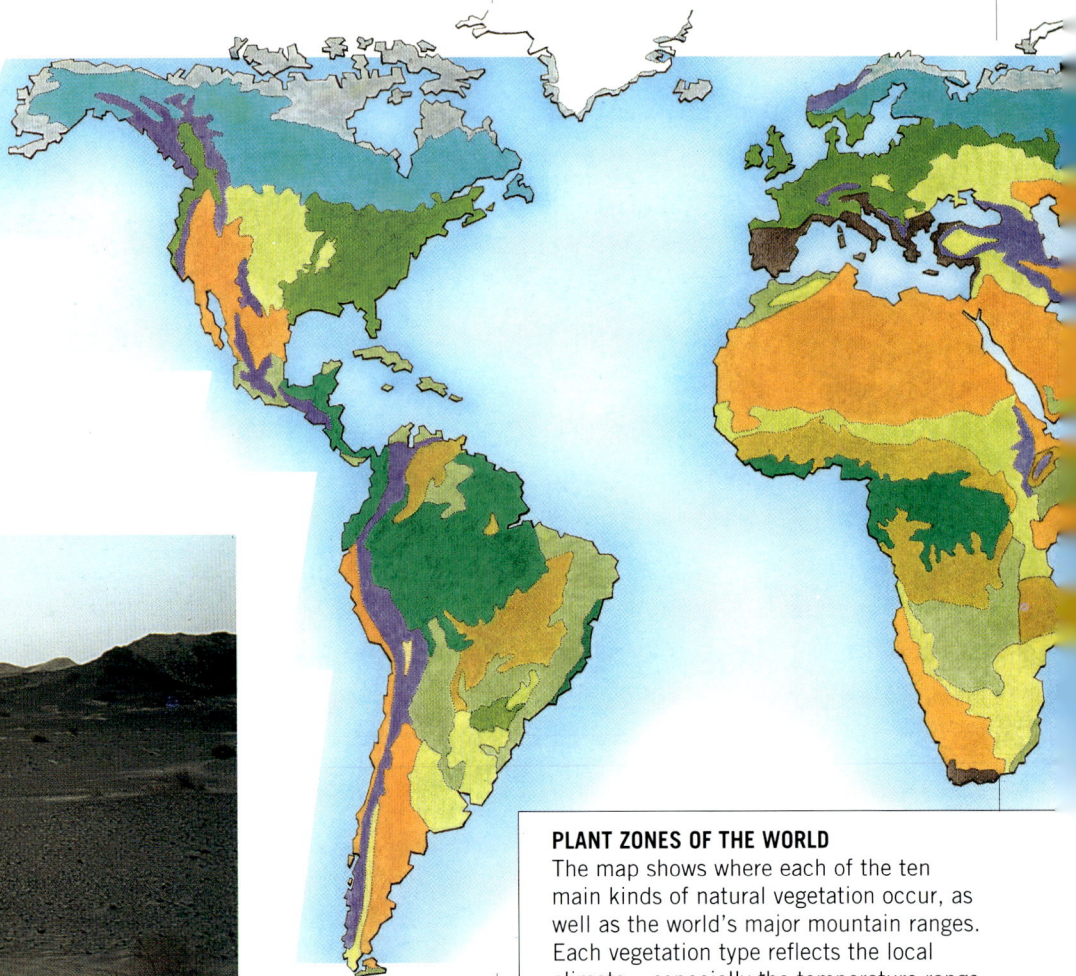

Sparse, scrubby vegetation is typical of the landscape in much of North Africa, as here in northern Tokar, Sudan.

PLANT ZONES OF THE WORLD
The map shows where each of the ten main kinds of natural vegetation occur, as well as the world's major mountain ranges. Each vegetation type reflects the local climate – especially the temperature range and rainfall patterns – and, to a lesser extent, the type of soil and the nature of the local landforms.

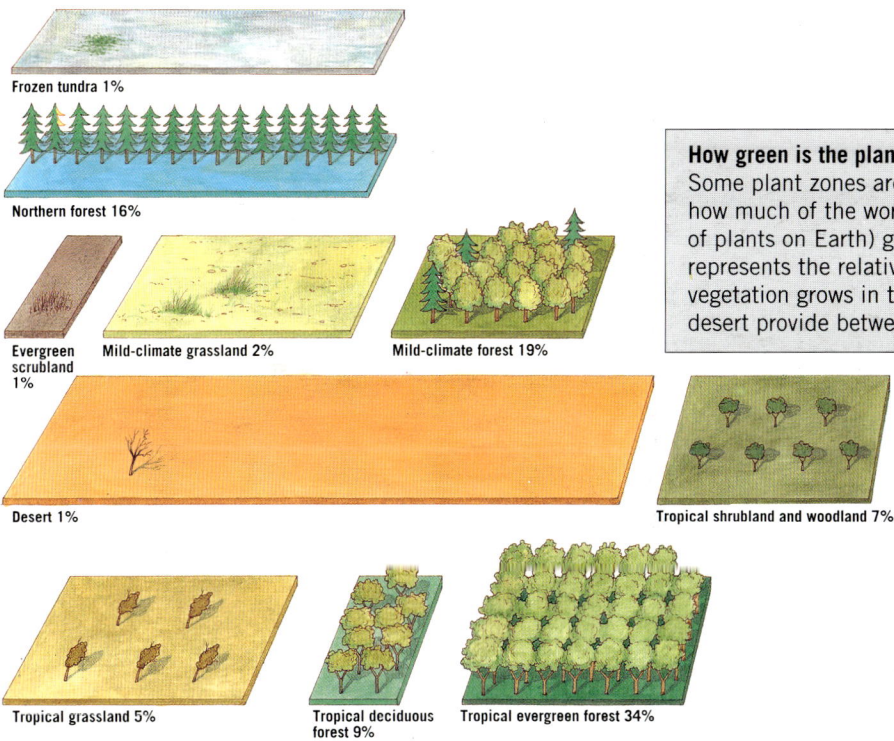

Frozen tundra 1%

Northern forest 16%

Evergreen scrubland 1%

Mild-climate grassland 2%

Mild-climate forest 19%

Desert 1%

Tropical shrubland and woodland 7%

Tropical grassland 5%

Tropical deciduous forest 9%

Tropical evergreen forest 34%

How green is the planet?
Some plant zones are much more fertile than others. The diagram shows how much of the world's vegetation (as a percentage of the total weight of plants on Earth) grows in each plant zone. The size of each block represents the relative land area of the zone. The largest share of vegetation grows in tropical rainforests. The huge areas of tundra and desert provide between them only one-fiftieth of the world's plant matter.

The weight of plants
If all the living things on Earth – plants, animals, algae, fungi, and **bacteria** – could be weighed, 99 per cent of the total weight would be plants. The weight of living material is called **biomass**. Forests contain more than three-quarters of all land biomass. Although tropical forests cover less than a tenth of the planet's surface, they contain more than half of the land biomass. Farmers' crops make up only about 0.5 per cent of the total weight of living plants.

Plants grow fastest in tropical forests, which account for nearly a quarter of new plant growth every year. Regions in the **tropics** produce new plant material more than twice as quickly as mild-climate zones, and more than four times as fast as northern forests.

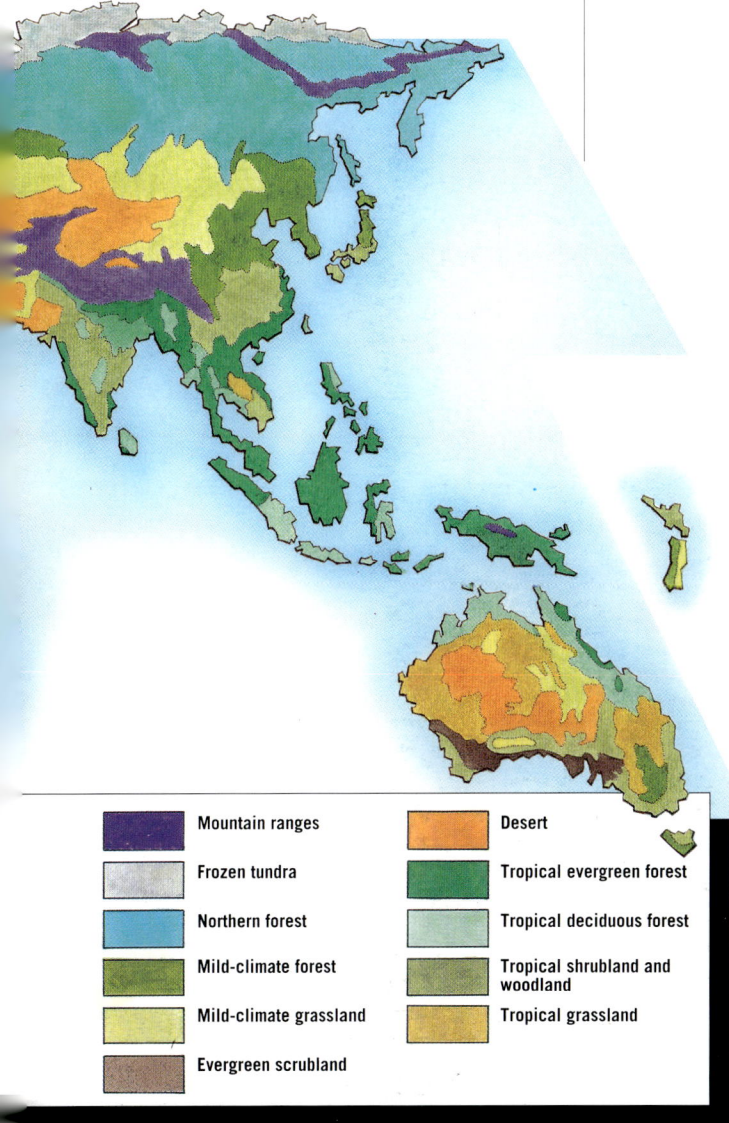

Understanding plant zones
The frozen **tundra** is close to the Arctic: few plants grow there. The northern forests of Canada, Europe, and North Asia have **coniferous** (cone-bearing) trees. Mild-climate forests, found mainly in North America, Europe, and North and East Asia, have a mixture of evergreen and **deciduous** (leaf-shedding) trees.

Mild-climate grasslands include the plains of North and South America, Central Asia, and South Africa. The dry evergreen scrubland zones of the southern USA, Mexico, and southern Europe have short, tough plants. The world's deserts – in the Americas, Africa, the Middle East, Central Asia, and Australia – are very dry zones where few plants survive.

The jungles of Central and South America, Central Africa, and Southeast Asia are tropical evergreen rain-forest. In Southeast Asia's tropical deciduous forest, trees lose their leaves during the dry season. Tropical shrub and wood-land have fewer trees and more open space than trop-ical forest. Tropical grass-land has even fewer trees.

Legend
- Mountain ranges
- Frozen tundra
- Northern forest
- Mild-climate forest
- Mild-climate grassland
- Evergreen scrubland
- Desert
- Tropical evergreen forest
- Tropical deciduous forest
- Tropical shrubland and woodland
- Tropical grassland

Photosynthesis and energy
Plant growth depends on a process called photosynthesis (literally, "building with light"). A green substance in the leaves – **chlorophyll** – absorbs energy from sunlight. Plants use this energy to combine carbon dioxide gas from the air, water from the soil, and small amounts of other chemicals to make carbohydrates, which include sugars and starch. From carbohydrates plants make fats and **proteins**, which are needed by them to stay alive. During the process of photosynthesis, plants give off oxygen into the air. Large areas of vegetation are therefore very good regulators of oxygen and carbon dioxide levels in the atmosphere.

GLOBAL FOREST

Forests and woodlands are one of the planet's greatest natural resources. They provide us with wood to make into paper and to use as a fuel for cooking and heating, and as a building material. They even supply us with substances to make into medicines. Forests are also host to an enormous variety of animals and plants.

HOME ACTION

We need more trees everywhere, and trees need friends. Here are some ways in which you can help.

● Care for trees by watering them during dry weather and clearing away any weeds around them.
● Tell your local authority if you think somebody is going to damage or destroy a tree.
● Learn more about trees.
● Collect seeds such as acorns, and raise seedlings in your own tree nursery.
● Plant native trees in your garden, at your school or community centre, or on patches of waste ground.
● Buy or sponsor a tree for somebody as a birthday or anniversary present.
● Support an organization that campaigns to protect and plant trees.

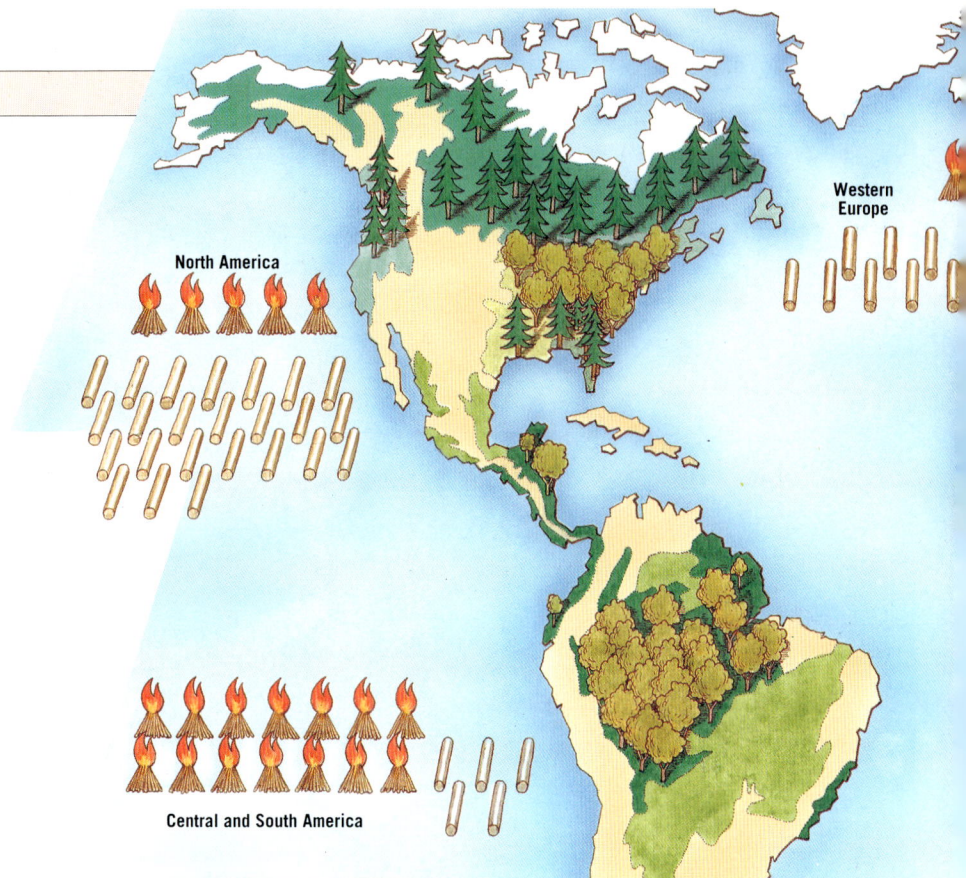

North America

Western Europe

Central and South America

FOREST LANDS AND USES OF WOOD

The world's main forest areas cover at least a fifth of the land. Broad-leaved trees make up more than half the planet's forests. Coniferous trees, such as pines, which have needle-shaped leaves, grow mainly in far northern regions.

The fuelwood and log symbols show how much wood people use for fuel and for industry (for example, in building and paper making) in a year in each continent or region. Together, the symbols show the amount of wood cut down every year. Developing countries use most of the fuelwood, while developed countries use most wood for industry.

Northern forest (mainly conifers)

Tropical evergreen rainforest and deciduous forest

Mild-climate mixed forest (conifers and broad-leaved trees)

Open dry woodland

Mild-climate broad-leaved forest

Coniferous forest: 20 million ha

Broad-leaved forest: 20 million ha

Fuelwood: 20 million m^3 each year

Wood for industry: 20 million m^3 each year

Forests and woodlands cover about a quarter of the planet's land surface, ranging from the huge tropical rainforests of the Amazon in South America, to the equally impressive forests of coniferous (cone-bearing) trees in Siberia, North Asia. The Earth's forests contain the richest variety of plants and animals anywhere on land, and the oldest and largest living things – trees. Oak, redwood, and yew trees live for hundreds, sometimes thousands, of years. They may tower above us, or have trunks large enough for people to live in. Tropical forests are sometimes millions of years old.

Eastern Europe
and former
Soviet Union

East Asia

Middle East

South and
Southeast Asia

Oceania

Africa

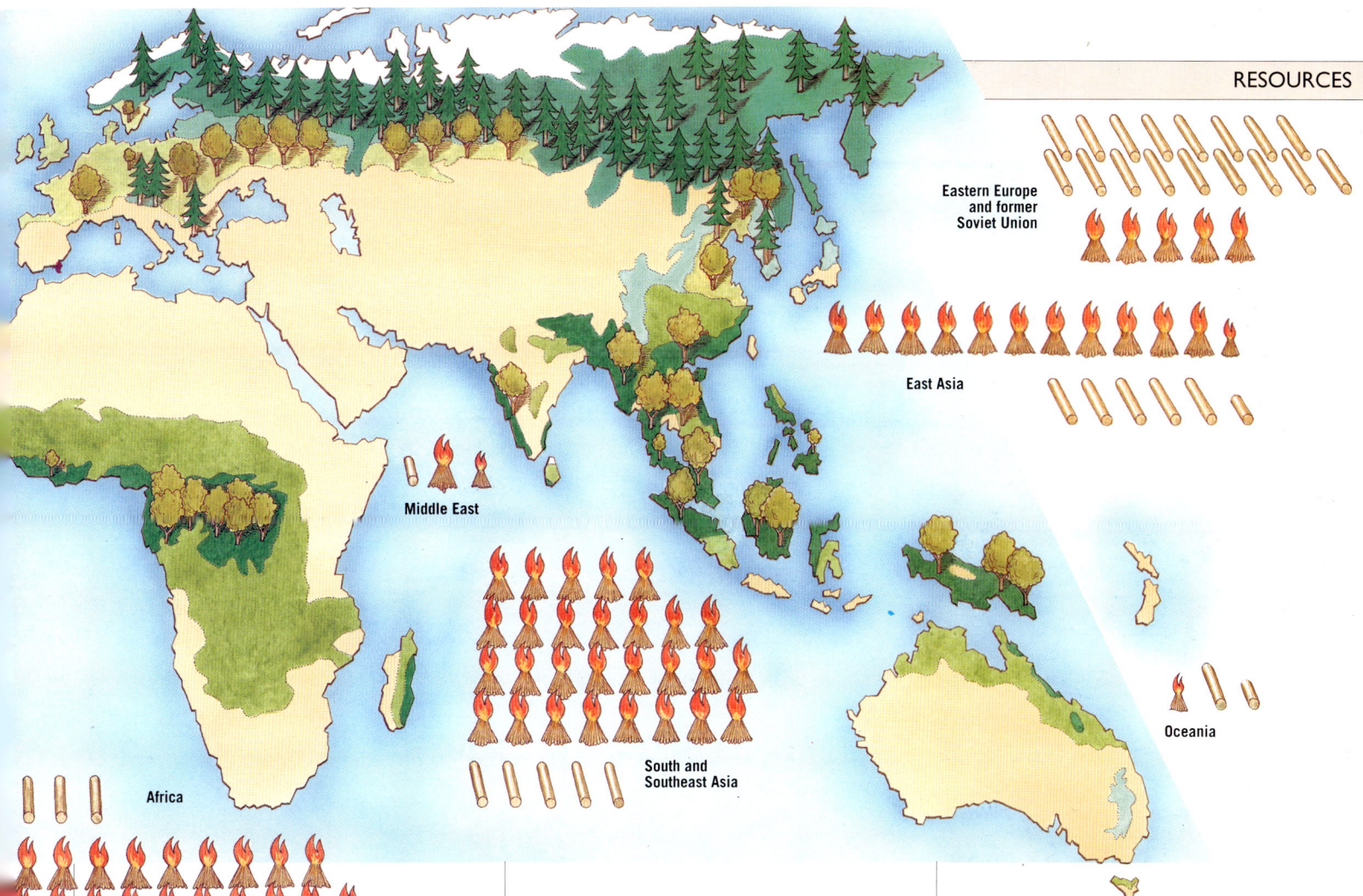

The value of trees

Besides being impressive in their own right, forests and their trees are important in very many ways. They are the world's great centres of photosynthesis, the process by which all plants grow. The roots and leaves of trees transport water from the soil to the air, helping to maintain a climate suitable for other living things, and to clean polluted air. They protect the soil from erosion and overheating, and feed it with their falling leaves. They protect the sources of rivers and help to prevent flooding. Finally, they shelter the nesting and breeding sites of many animal species, as well as being home to about 200 million people throughout the world.

Wood is essential to many aspects of our lives and probably more important for human civilization than any other material. Without it, we could not make all the paper we need. Trees provide **fuelwood** for cooking and heating for about half the world's people. Less energy is needed to work with wood than cement, plastic, or metal. The walls of a wooden house provide better insulation (preventing heat escaping and cold air entering) than most other materials. Many everyday things that we take for granted – medicines such as aspirin, for example – also come from trees.

Forests hold secrets that we have yet to discover. Who knows how many new plant and animal species, and new uses for forest products, people will discover in the future – if forests survive?

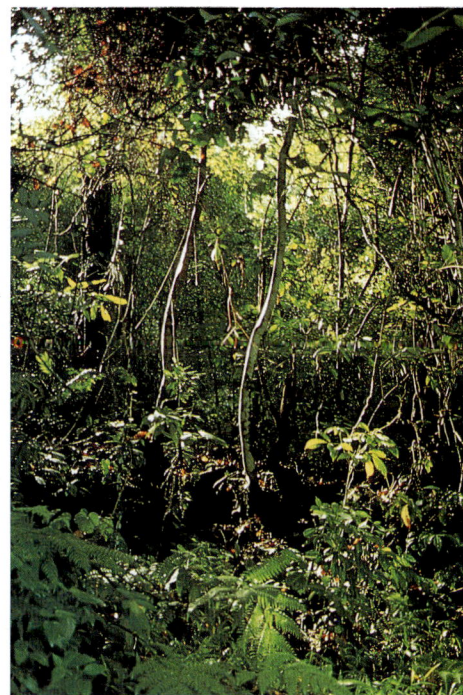

Tropical rainforest in Indonesia displays the many levels of plant life that are typical of this vegetation zone.

SHRINKING FORESTS

As you read this page, an area of tropical rainforest larger than an Olympic Games sports stadium is being destroyed – by burning, being hacked down tree by tree with a chain saw, or being bulldozed out of existence. Most people agree that this destruction is wrong, but so far nobody has managed to stop it.

Every year people destroy about 17 million hectares of tropical forest and woodland – an area twice the size of Austria – and badly damage another five million hectares or more of tropical forest. Worldwide, trees are disappearing ten times faster than people plant them.

People everywhere want more wood. In developing countries the main need is for fuelwood, and local communities take what they need for their own use. These developing countries also use their tropical forests to earn much-needed money. They sell timber to developed countries, which use enormous quantities for building and in **industry**. Even if big businesses, rather than local people, cut down the trees using careful methods of **forestry**, they can still cause serious damage.

Forest that has lost most, but not all, of its trees can usually grow back, given enough time. But this process may take 100 years or more, and often it is not given a chance. Once a **logging** company has built roads into the forest, poor people who have nowhere to live,

or richer people greedy for more land, may move in and clear the remaining trees. All these activities also threaten the lives of the original forest people.

The need for wood does not tell the whole story. Huge areas of tropical forest disappear when countries build giant dams, set up large mining operations, or clear land for commercial farming. Most of these activities happen because developing countries see them as a way of making themselves richer. Yet these activities cause more problems than they solve.

Will forests survive?
The area of land covered by forest has shrunk dramatically during the last 45 years. In 1950, forest covered almost a third of the Earth's land surface, divided equally between tropical forest and mild-climate forest. By 1975, the area of tropical forest was noticeably smaller. By the end of the century, tropical forest will probably cover only a third of the area it covered 50 years ago. Forest in mild-climate regions has stayed about the same, mainly because the richer, developed countries of these zones are better able to protect and replant their trees than the developing countries of tropical regions.

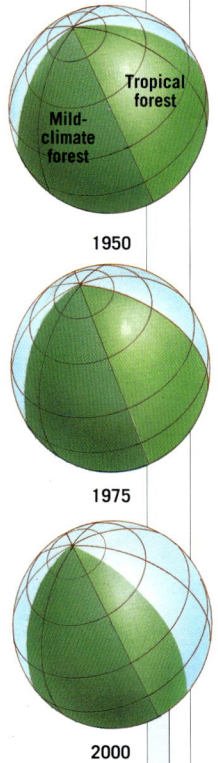

Tropical forest / Mild-climate forest / 1950 / 1975 / 2000

FORESTS UNDER ATTACK
The red zones show where human activity is destroying forests fastest. Forests are most at risk in Central and South America, Central Africa, South and Southeast Asia, and eastern Australia.

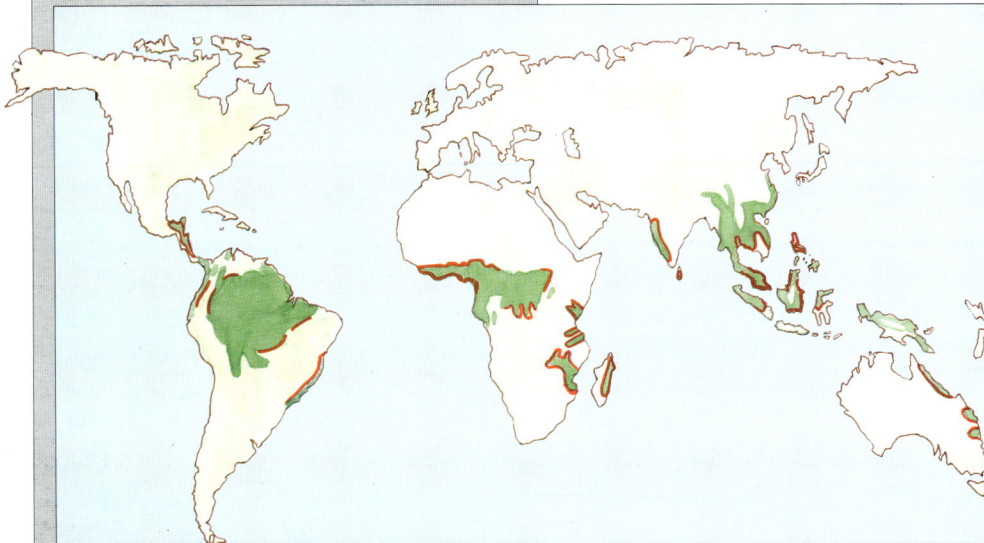

Cattle graze in Amazonas, *Brazil, on land once covered with trees.*

When the forests have gone

Tropical forest soils are unsuitable either for growing crops or raising cattle. Once the trees have gone, the heavy rains typical of these regions wash nutrients out of the soils, and there are no longer falling leaves to feed them. The soils become tired and useless after just a few years of heavy farming.

Sometimes land never recovers from forest destruction. Stripped bare, the soil may bake to a hard, dry crust. In hilly or mountainous areas, the loss of trees can cause landslides, burying people alive or sweeping away their homes. With the trees gone, rivers may not flow as steadily. Their courses and volume of water may vary, causing floods, such as those that have killed hundreds of thousands of people in Bangladesh. Cities that depend on river water may find their supplies running dangerously low, as in some developing countries today, and local climates may change. The low rainfall in Africa in recent years may be connected to the loss of tree cover.

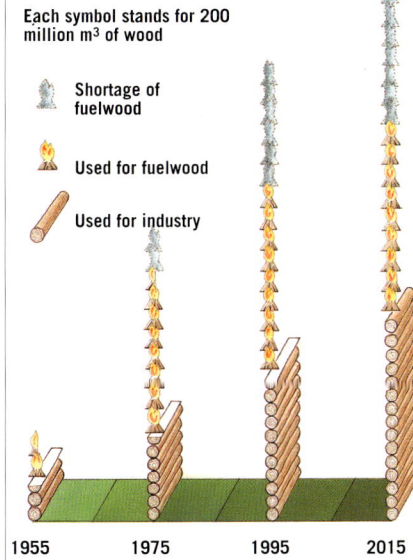

Each symbol stands for 200 million m³ of wood

Shortage of fuelwood

Used for fuelwood

Used for industry

| 1955 | 1975 | 1995 | 2015 |

WOOD CONSUMPTION

In 1955, more wood was used for building, paper making, and other industrial uses (log symbol) than for fuel (fuelwood symbol). Fuelwood took a larger share 20 years later. As **consumption** increases and wood becomes scarcer (dotted symbol), people use animal dung and crop remains as fuel. By 2015, the fuelwood shortage will be serious.

Making use of wood, North and South

In the developed countries of the northern hemisphere, wood is processed to make paper, packaging, household items, and building materials. Many products are used, then discarded. People in the South use a lot of wood as fuel and for building. They use far less paper (because of its high cost) and conserve wood products more.

Everybody's loss

The large-scale burning of forests releases carbon dioxide gas into the air and removes trees that absorb carbon dioxide (during photosynthesis), almost certainly adding to the problem of **global warming** (the worldwide increase in surface temperatures). Forest destruction also spells danger – perhaps extinction – for many animal and plant species, and it threatens people who live in the forests and depend on them for survival. For all of us, it means that our planet is losing some of its most wonderful natural riches.

21

SOIL LOSS

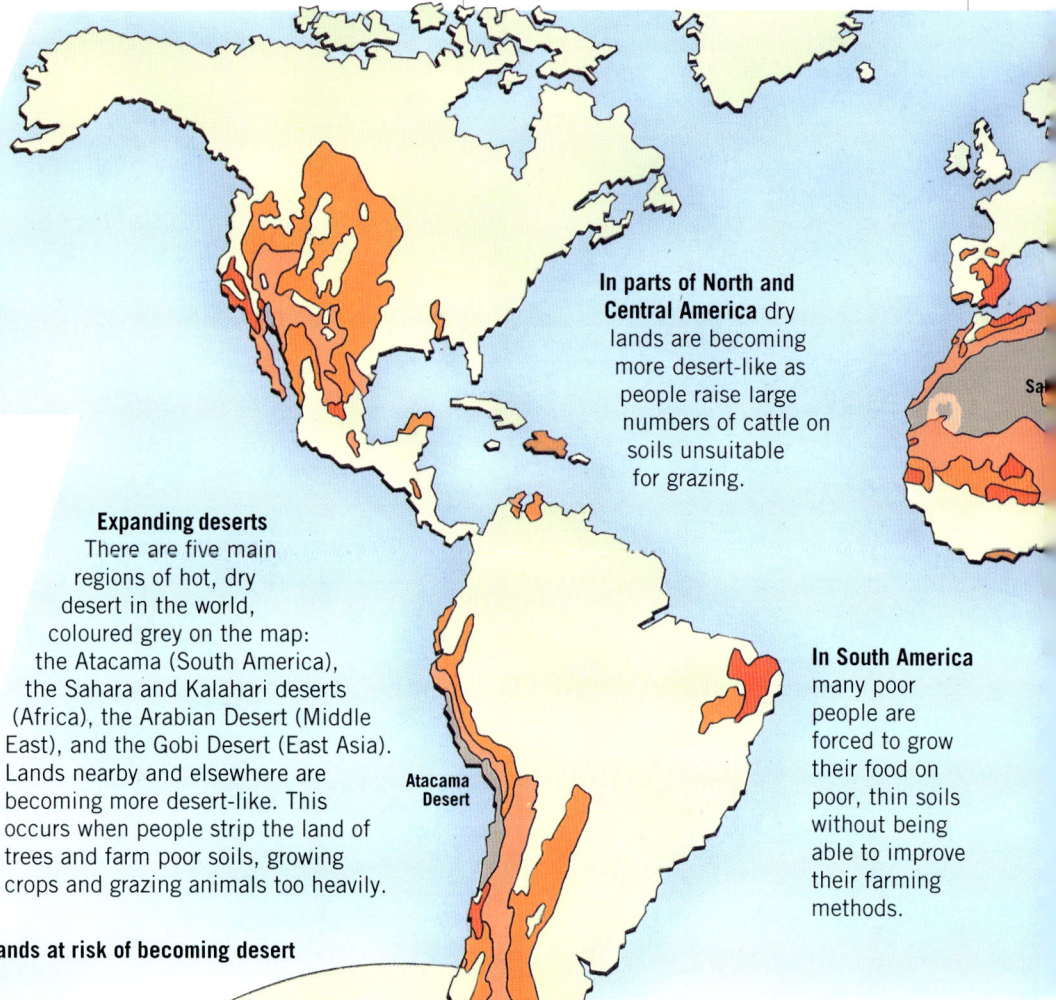

Sand can be fun at the seaside, and it has its uses in industry. But if you have ever tried to grow plants in sand, or have been in a sandstorm, you will know that if all our soil turned to sand we would be in serious trouble.

DID YOU KNOW?

Rivers build islands
A large landmass is forming under the sea in the Bay of Bengal, south of Bangladesh, as a result of trees being chopped down on the lower slopes of mountains hundreds of kilometres away. Every year, thousands of tonnes of topsoil are washed off the Himalayan mountainsides and hills, and carried by the Brahmaputra and Ganges rivers across India and Bangladesh to the bay. The landmass will surface above sea level in about 15 years.

In parts of North and Central America dry lands are becoming more desert-like as people raise large numbers of cattle on soils unsuitable for grazing.

Expanding deserts
There are five main regions of hot, dry desert in the world, coloured grey on the map: the Atacama (South America), the Sahara and Kalahari deserts (Africa), the Arabian Desert (Middle East), and the Gobi Desert (East Asia). Lands nearby and elsewhere are becoming more desert-like. This occurs when people strip the land of trees and farm poor soils, growing crops and grazing animals too heavily.

Lands at risk of becoming desert

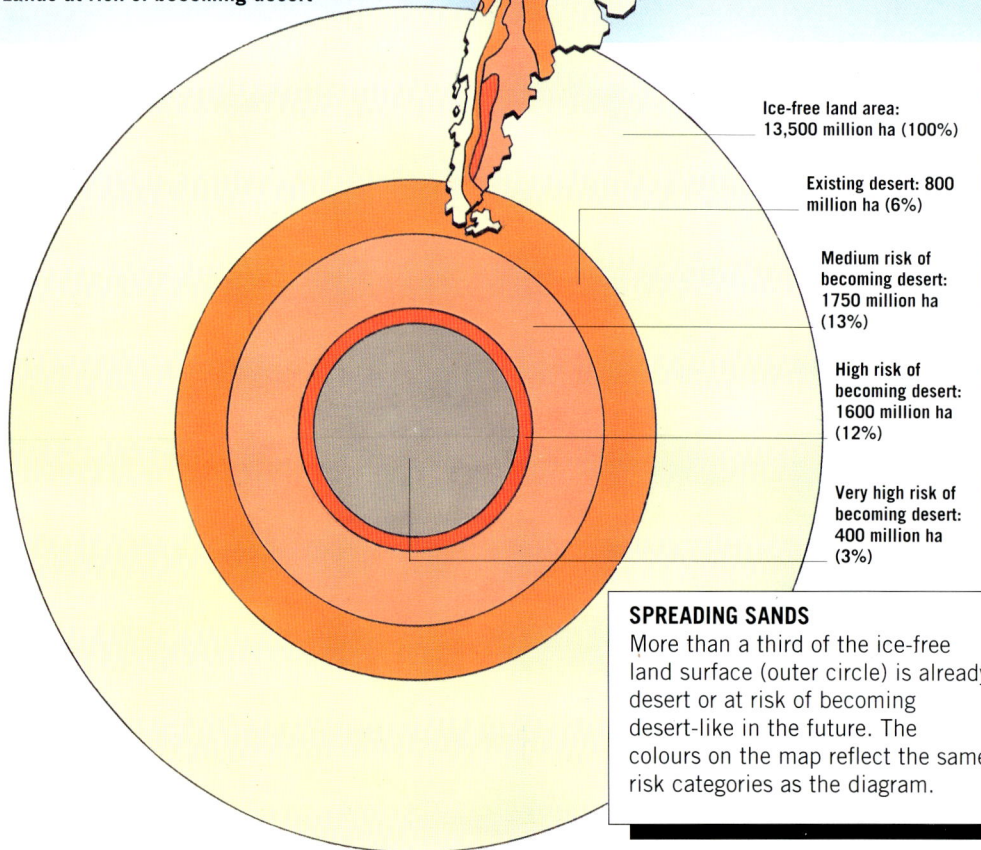

In South America many poor people are forced to grow their food on poor, thin soils without being able to improve their farming methods.

Atacama Desert

Ice-free land area: 13,500 million ha (100%)

Existing desert: 800 million ha (6%)

Medium risk of becoming desert: 1750 million ha (13%)

High risk of becoming desert: 1600 million ha (12%)

Very high risk of becoming desert: 400 million ha (3%)

SPREADING SANDS
More than a third of the ice-free land surface (outer circle) is already desert or at risk of becoming desert-like in the future. The colours on the map reflect the same risk categories as the diagram.

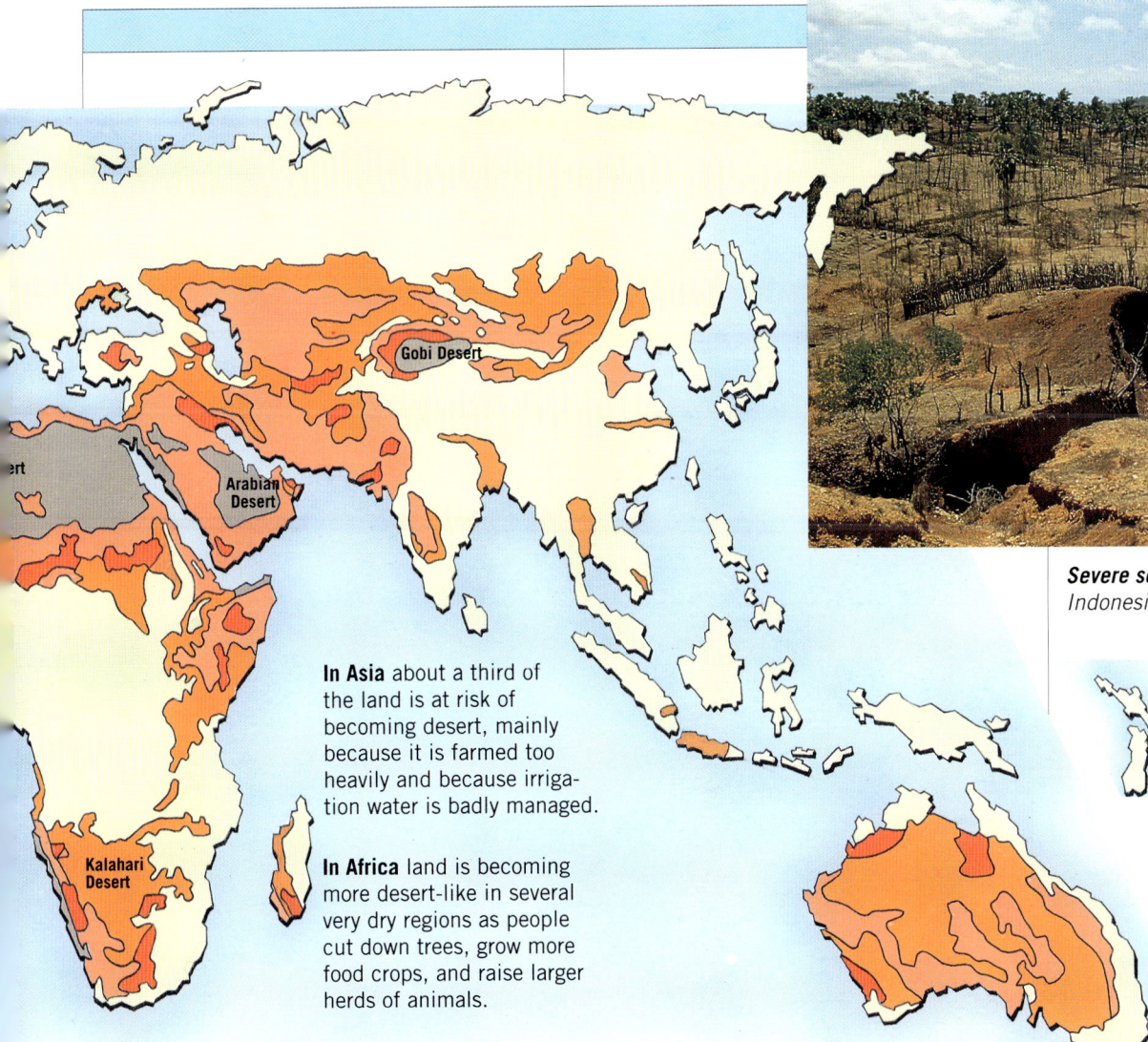

Severe soil erosion in parts of Sabu Island, Indonesia.

Gobi Desert

Arabian Desert

Kalahari Desert

In Asia about a third of the land is at risk of becoming desert, mainly because it is farmed too heavily and because irrigation water is badly managed.

In Africa land is becoming more desert-like in several very dry regions as people cut down trees, grow more food crops, and raise larger herds of animals.

In Australia the increase in desert conditions is happening only very slowly, but in much of the country grazing animals are seriously damaging the land.

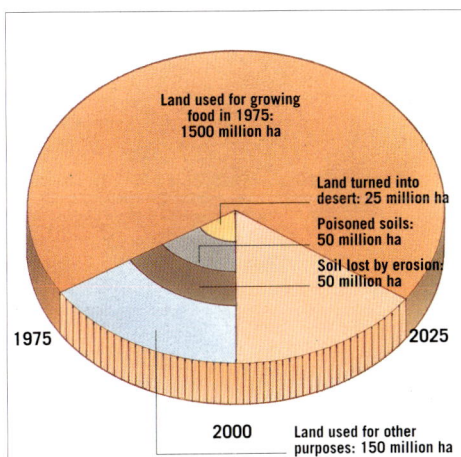

Land used for growing food in 1975: 1500 million ha

Land turned into desert: 25 million ha

Poisoned soils: 50 million ha

Soil lost by erosion: 50 million ha

1975   2025

2000   Land used for other purposes: 150 million ha

Vanishing farmland
By the year 2000, we may have lost almost a fifth of the land on which we grew food in 1975 (represented by the full circle), and who knows how much more by 2025? The main causes are the spread of deserts, soils harmed by salt and chemicals, wind and rain erosion, and changing land use.

The Earth's land surface is losing soil at a frighteningly fast rate. Every year, wind and rain erode millions of tonnes of earth worldwide, blowing it into the air or washing it into rivers, and finally dumping it in lakes and oceans, from where it cannot be recovered. This affects tropical regions more than others. Ethiopia, for example, loses as much topsoil each year as the USA, which is six times larger.

The stripping of trees and other natural protection against wind and rain can lead to soil erosion. Seasonal flooding or the drying of local climates can also increase the risk of erosion. Farmers add to the risk by grazing large herds of animals on poor soils or by using

chemicals and machines that damage the soil. Farmland also suffers when farmers use **irrigation** (artificial watering) without good drainage. Soils may become waterlogged or damaged by salt and other chemicals.

In dry zones, large areas are becoming of poorer quality and therefore less suitable for cultivation. This is known as "**dryland degradation**" or "**desertification**". It happens when people try to grow more crops than the dry, semi-desert soils can feed, or graze more animals on the land than it can support. The loss of land for growing crops was one cause of the famines in Africa's Sahel region in the 1970s and 1980s.

SEA DYKES IN VIETNAM

Every year the coast of Vietnam is lashed by tropical storms and typhoons. The area around Ky Anh, in central Vietnam, suffers badly, with the loss of lives, homes, crops, and animals. There is barely time to recover before the next typhoon season begins.

Nguyen Van Tu has vivid memories of Typhoon Becky, which struck in 1990: "All we could do when we saw how the sea was rising was to pick up our children and set out into the darkness towards dry land. I had to force my way through water that was up to my neck in places."

The rice paddies of Ky Anh lie in the narrow area of land between the mountains and the sea. Often they are flooded by the sea, making the soil salty and infertile. It takes years for the soil to recover, so there are often food shortages.

The long coastline of Vietnam is constantly battered by storms, during which the sea used to flood low-lying farmland between the coast and the mountains. Paddy fields and vegetable and fruit crops were destroyed.

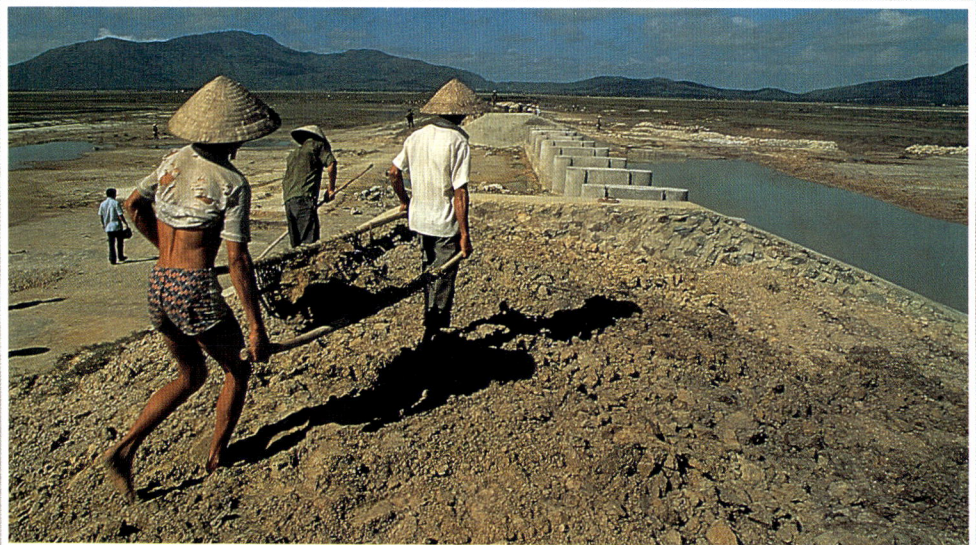

▲ *People carried soil to the site, where it was pressed firmly into position by machine. The slope facing the sea was covered with large rocks to protect it from waves. The landward slope was planted with grass.*

An early-warning system helps to save lives, but the people of Ky Anh needed something to protect their land.

The answer was to build **dykes** along the coast to hold back the sea and protect the valuable soil. There had been dykes in the area before, but they had been bombed during the Vietnam War (1965–73) and neglected since. Now they were easily breached by the sea.

Redesign and a rebuilding programme were much needed.

Help arrived in the form of engineers from Hanoi Water Resources University, who assessed the problems and designed a better, stronger dyke. They trained local people in new building methods. The work was done by teams of volunteers, working on the dyke nearest their community. Along much of the

length of the dykes on the seaward side, communities are planting **mangroves**. These will provide extra protection against the waves.

By 1995 nearly half the 65 kilometres of dykes had been rebuilt, protecting more than 35,000 people and their land. It will be 1999 before the soil has completely recovered, but people are able to plant crops again, knowing they are safe from the sea.

▲ *Once local technicians* and workteam leaders had been trained, some 3000 people from local communities set to work rebuilding the 17-kilometre-long embankment.

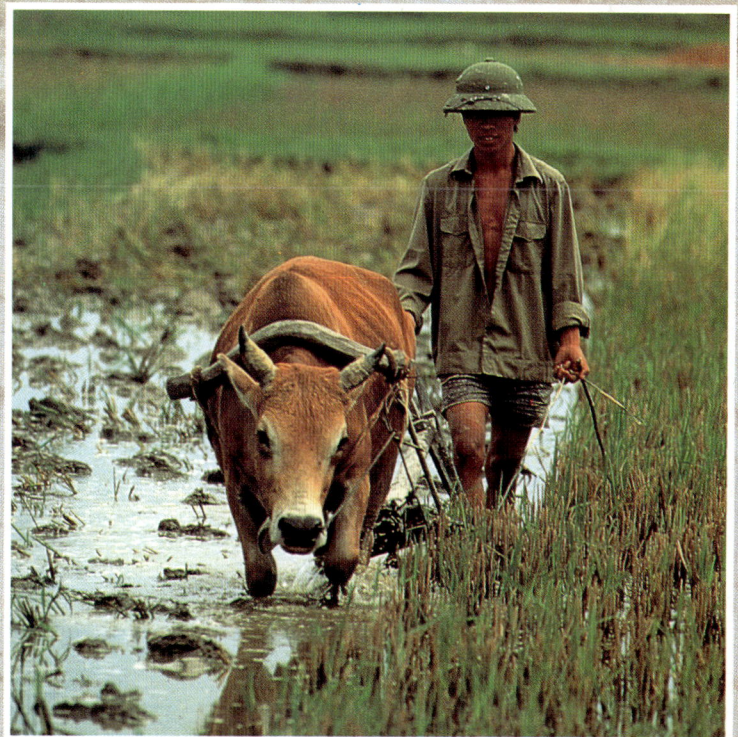

▶ *Rice is the most important crop* in Ky Anh. Flooding used to leave the paddy fields full of salt. This caused low crop yields, which meant food shortages for the people of Ky Anh.

GOOD USE OF LAND

If you have ever been in the open countryside on a hot day, you will know how important a shady tree can be. Trees need soil to grow in, and people need soil and woodland to survive. There are important ways to make sure that future generations have plenty of both.

Penan forest people protest against commercial logging in the rainforest of Sarawak in Malaysia.

One of the best ways to protect land and forests is to help local people look after them. Damage to soil and trees often happens when local people lose control over their land, such as when a government or company wants to clear land to grow food, usually to sell abroad.

Some people argue that the protection of forests in developed countries is less of a problem, as these countries can buy wood from abroad. By **recycling** paper and using less tropical **hardwoods**, however, developed countries can help conserve trees worldwide.

In developing countries, local people who have a fair share of the use of forests look after them well. Many governments encourage local people to protect the forests and replant them, using multipurpose trees that provide fuelwood, food for animals, building timber, and other useful materials. Replanting bare hillsides with trees helps stop floods and landslides, and stabilizes streams and rivers.

Community forest   Villagers' homes   Animal manure enriches the soil   Small dam controls irrigation water

Good soils allow people to grow a wide range of food crops, especially if they irrigate them with water, raise different crops together – often in the same field – and rotate (change around) the crops in each field each year. **Organic** material, such as crop remains and animal manure, enriches the soil. Trees and hedges (including fruit- and nut-producing varieties) can grow among the fields.

Medium-quality land is most suitable for crops such as **pulses** (peas and beans) and sweetcorn. Farmers can grow peanut and cowpea (a tropical climbing **legume** with long pods containing pea-like seeds), which put goodness back in the soil as well as providing fodder (food) for animals. Poorer-quality soils need **fallow** (rest) periods between plantings of crops to allow them to recover.

Community forest

In Kenya, India, and many other developing countries, local people are involved in raising seedlings and setting up plantations of new multipurpose trees. Many schemes are supported by international **development** agencies. Local people are often the best protectors of existing forest in and around their village, as long as they can use it for their own needs.

On hillsides farmers can build **terraces** (narrow, flat areas, stepped up the slope) on which they grow crops. Terracing prevents the creep of soil downhill. Small numbers of hardy breeds of sheep and goats can graze dry hillsides without causing damage.

Conserving the environment

Local people need help from governments to prevent soil erosion and the spread of deserts. Some need money and machinery, others the advice of agricultural scientists or engineers. Planting trees, using irrigation on a small scale, **organic farming** (without artificial chemicals), and choosing the right crops and animals for their land, all help to conserve that land and create jobs.

If damaged or overused land is to recover, people in developed countries should not demand too much for themselves, while those in developing countries must have what they need to survive.

LOOKING AFTER THE LAND

This landscape, set in an imaginary developing country, shows ways of making good use of the land, while at the same time preventing the loss of soil and the spread of desert. The landscape ranges from fertile cropland (in the far left of the diagram) to dry, almost lifeless desert (far right). In each area – except for the natural desert, which people usually cannot farm – a good choice of crops and careful methods help farmers conserve and maintain healthy soil.

Dry grassland is better for grazing animals than growing crops. If people raise animals just to serve local needs, and move the herds from one place to another, the land is unlikely to become overgrazed and the soil poor. Planting clover and other such grasses feeds the soil. Carefully chosen tree species provide fuelwood and extra animal **fodder**, and protect the soil from erosion.

Rows of trees planted along tracks and roads protect the land from wind and rain, and provide other useful products, including firewood. At the edge of the natural desert (to the right of the diagram), suitable hardy trees and shrubs, including those that supply rubber, wax, and wood, will hold back the spread of the sand dunes and make the best use of poor-quality land.

FOOD AND FARMING

"Give me an oak forest and I will give you pots full of milk and baskets full of grain."

Song of women in Reni, northern India, who are protecting forests

The demands made by ever-increasing numbers of people on the world's farming have created a range of problems. Modern farming methods damage the soil and use up precious resources, such as fresh water that has taken thousands of years to collect in underground rocks. Large-scale, commercial farming makes some people enormously rich and overfeeds many on unhealthy diets, while leaving millions of others homeless, poor, and hungry. It relies on chemicals that pollute our world and depends on resources that may not last another century. It has led to a huge loss of wild species worldwide and to large areas of countryside becoming near-lifeless deserts or open-air food-production factories. But help is at hand in the form of different – but not always new – ways of growing our food. Can we meet the challenge and make the future of farming a success for everyone?

Large-scale, highly mechanized "prairie" wheat farming can cause severe soil erosion, and creates very few jobs.

CROPS & CROPLANDS

Much of what we eat today will become part of our bodies tomorrow; and, apart from fish and seafood, it all comes from the land. Using the land wisely is therefore as important as looking after our physical health, because unhealthy land cannot produce good food. How healthy is the land today and how much food can we grow on it?

DID YOU KNOW?

What are cereals?
All **cereal** crops are members of the grass family of plants. People grow them for their large edible seed-heads, called **grains**, which provide over half the food energy in the human diet. People use cereals in many different ways. We can cook them (rice, for example) or grind them into flour to make pasta or bread (wheat and rye, for example). We can give some grains, such as maize, barley, and oats, to animals to eat, and process others, including barley and rice, into cooking oils and drinks.

THE WORLD'S MAIN CROPS
Most of our food grows in the northern hemisphere. The lighter-coloured areas of the map show the location of the better croplands. Each food symbol represents a **harvest** of 10 million tonnes a year, and the different foods are identified at the foot of the page. Asia is the leading producer of wheat, rice, and pulses such as soya; Europe grows most potatoes; and North America produces most **maize** (sweet-corn). South America, Africa, and Oceania are less productive regions. The pie charts show how much land on each continent could be farmed, and how much actually is cultivated. Barrels and sacks represent quantities of **fertilizer** used and the size of harvests.

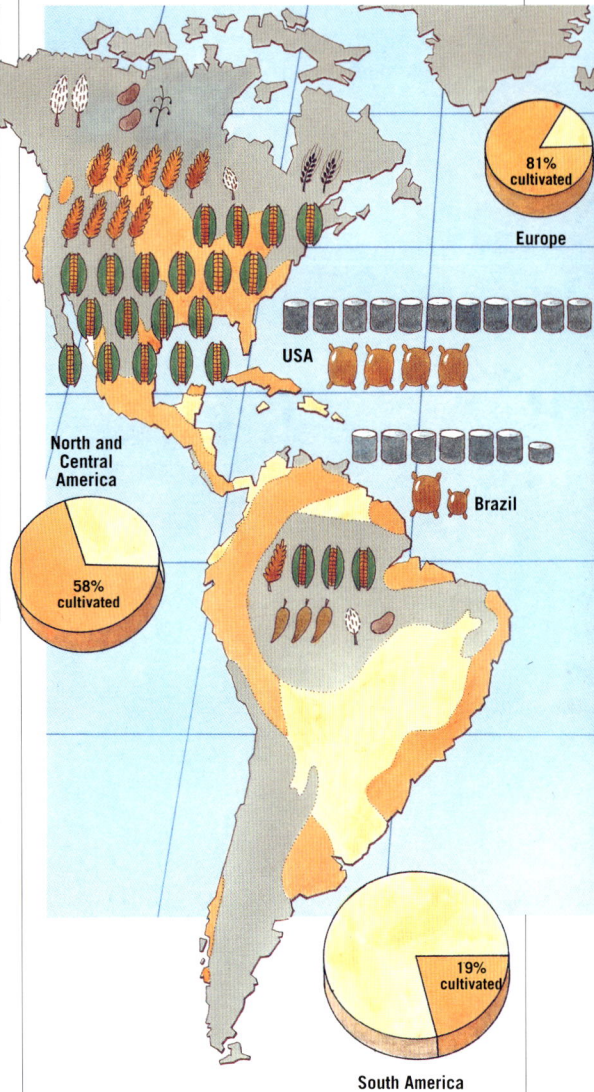

Farming began about 10,000 years ago in the Middle East and parts of Asia, as people started to settle along the river valleys and to **cultivate** crops and raise animals. This was one of the most important changes in human history. Croplands now cover 1500 million hectares worldwide (one-and-a-half times the area of the USA). Differences in soil and climate allow food crops to grow better in some places than in others. The milder climates and richer soils of much of Europe, North America, and Asia make them more suitable for farming than the dry, harsh conditions of much of Africa, the Middle East, and Oceania.

Modern technology can bring water to dry regions, and there are good traditional methods of making poor soils more fertile. But many people in developing countries cannot afford to pay for the improvements their land needs.

81% cultivated — Europe
USA
North and Central America — 58% cultivated
Brazil
19% cultivated — South America

Feeding the world

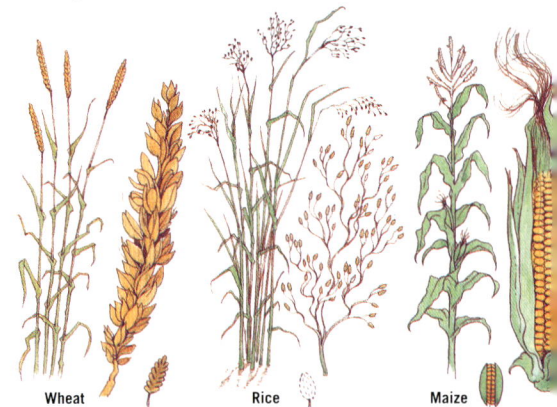

Wheat — Rice — Maize

Wheat, the world's biggest cereal crop, grows best in mild areas. **Rice** is Asia's main crop. By growing it in semi-flooded fields, farmers produce food all year. **Maize** (corn) is a major part of the diet in South America and Africa. Most US maize is fed to animals.

UK

Former Soviet Union

Former Soviet Union

65% cultivated

Japan

China

India

Nigeria

72% cultivated

Asia

30% cultivated

Oceania

25% cultivated

Africa

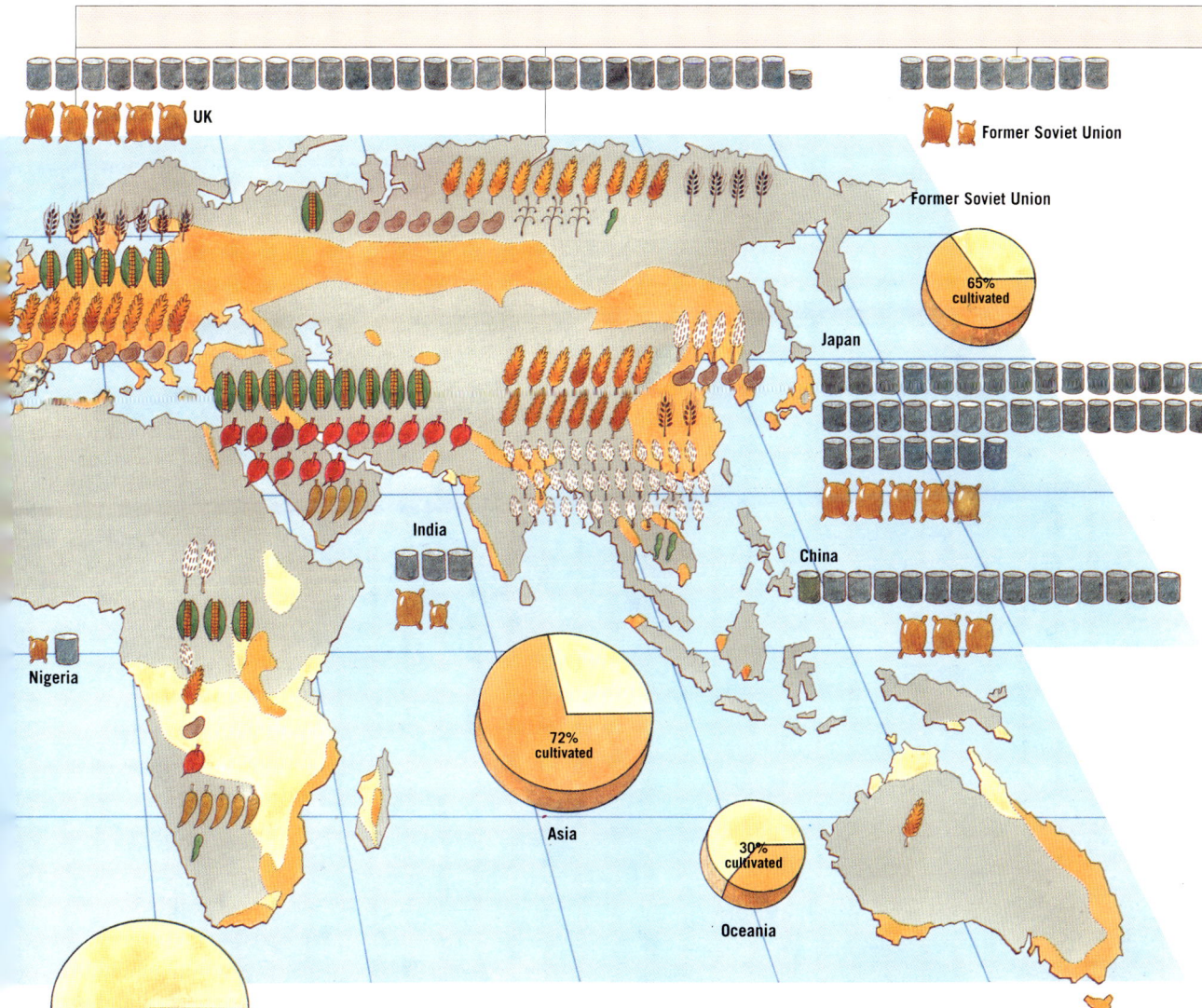

Land mainly used for crops, animal grazing, and forestry

Land that could be planted with crops, although needing improvement

Fertilizer input (10 kg per ha of cropland)

Cereal yield (tonnes per ha of cropland)

FERTILIZERS AND PRODUCTIVITY

Each oil barrel represents 10 kg of fertilizer used for every hectare of cropland. Each food sack represents 1 tonne of cereals grown on every hectare of cropland. We can compare farming methods worldwide. Brazil uses twice as much fertilizer as India to produce the same amount of cereals, because Indian farming is more skilful and labour-intensive. The UK and Japan, needing high **yields** from relatively small parcels of land, use very large amounts of fertilizer.

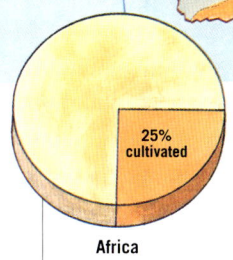

Using all the land

In North America, Europe, the former Soviet Union, and Asia most of the land that is suitable for farming is already being used. But in South America, Africa, and Oceania people could farm much more land than they now do, although some of this land would need to be improved first. Irrigation, tree planting, and the growing of deep-rooted plants would help upgrade the soil.

Potato

Barley

Sweet potato

Cassava

Sorghum/millet

Oats and rye

Pulses

Potatoes are swollen underground stems, not cereals. They grow best in cool, mild climates. **Barley,** a major cereal crop, is used mainly for animal feed and to make beer and whisky. **Sweet potatoes** grow in warm, damp areas of Africa, the Caribbean, and Asia.

Cassava – a root crop, not a cereal – grows well in dry climates, but is much less nutritious than most cereals. **Sorghum** and **millet,** two closely related cereals, grow well in hot, dry regions. The grains lack gluten and cannot be used for bread-making.

Oats and **rye** can be grown in both cool and damp climates. Oats are mainly fed to animals, and rye is used mostly for making bread. **Pulses** – beans and peas that form in pods – are important in developing countries. Soya beans are a major crop in Asia.

31

ANIMALS FOR FOOD

People all over the world rely on farm animals for meat, milk, and eggs that are rich in nutrients, as well as for other products such as wool. Worldwide, the area of land used by grazing (grass-eating) animals is double the area we use to grow crops, although some animals, such as goats, can survive on poor-quality food.

By converting plants that people cannot eat into useful energy, **domesticated** animals provide a valuable contribution to the human diet. Yet there are problems. Some grasslands are overgrazed: too many animals strip the land bare, making it vulnerable to erosion.

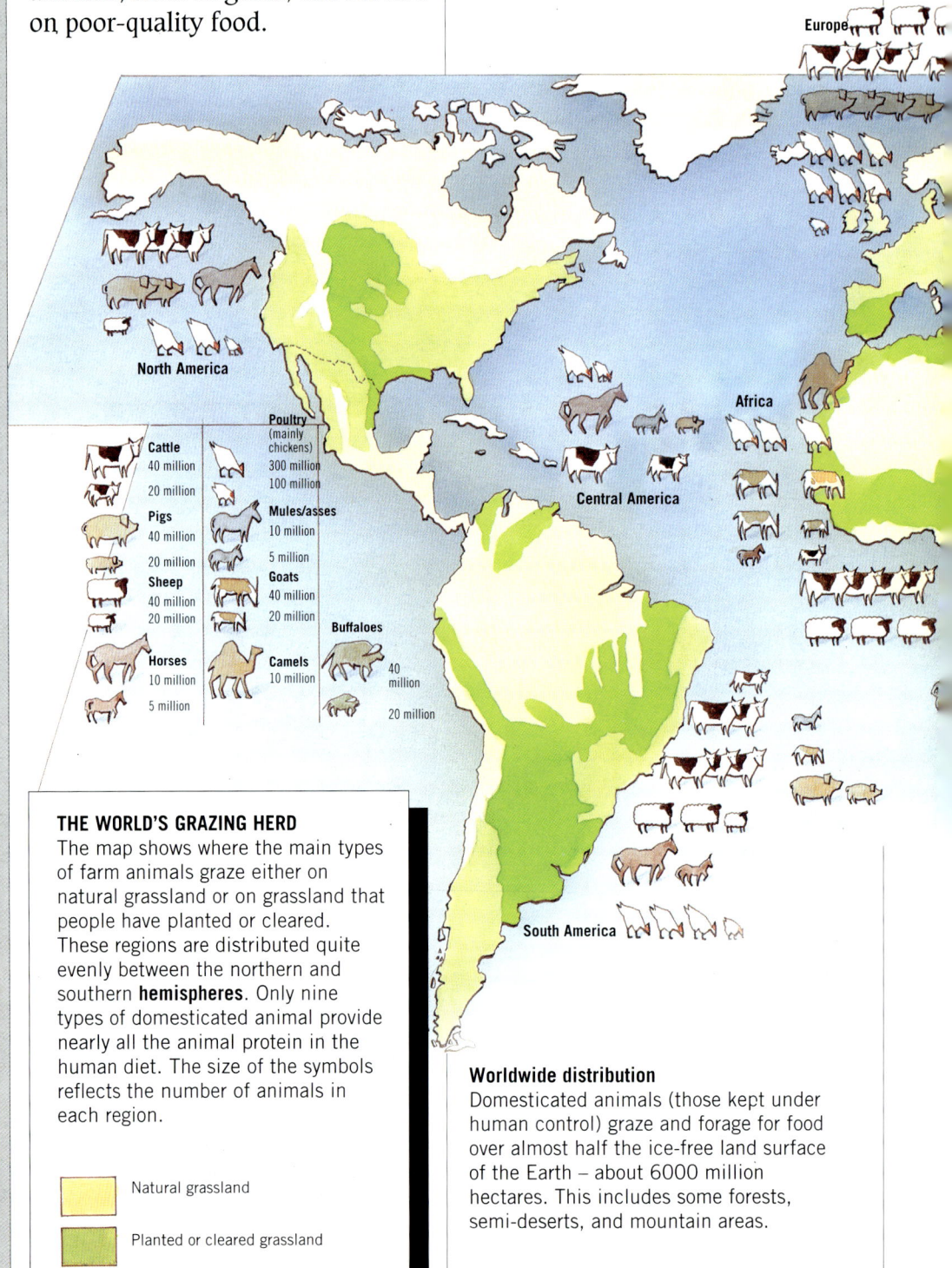

Do you like burgers? Lots of people do. In many countries the beef for burgers comes from cattle fed on soya. Much of the soya – which people, as well as cattle, can eat – is grown in Brazil, where hundreds of thousands of children go hungry. Raising animals for food brings benefits for many people, but problems for others.

On the high plains of Bolivia, llamas are reared for meat, milk, and hides.

THE WORLD'S GRAZING HERD
The map shows where the main types of farm animals graze either on natural grassland or on grassland that people have planted or cleared. These regions are distributed quite evenly between the northern and southern **hemispheres**. Only nine types of domesticated animal provide nearly all the animal protein in the human diet. The size of the symbols reflects the number of animals in each region.

Cattle 40 million / 20 million
Pigs 40 million / 20 million
Sheep 40 million / 20 million
Horses 10 million / 5 million
Poultry (mainly chickens) 300 million / 100 million
Mules/asses 10 million / 5 million
Goats 40 million / 20 million
Camels 10 million
Buffaloes 40 million / 20 million

Natural grassland
Planted or cleared grassland

Worldwide distribution
Domesticated animals (those kept under human control) graze and forage for food over almost half the ice-free land surface of the Earth – about 6000 million hectares. This includes some forests, semi-deserts, and mountain areas.

Animals reared intensively by "factory farming" not only lead confined lives, but often consume food that people could have eaten. Land used to provide meat for rich people far away could provide farms on which poor local people could grow their own food.

Former Soviet Union

DID YOU KNOW?

More chickens than people
There are 15,000 million domestic animals on Earth – almost three times the total number of people. They include 10,000 million chickens, 3000 million cows, sheep, goats, buffalo, camels, and llamas, and more than 850 million pigs. Two-thirds of the world's pigs live in China, and three out of every 20 cattle live in India.

Camel
Goat
Upland sheep
Free-range hen
Duck

Low-grade feeders, such as camels, goats, upland sheep, and free-range chickens, can survive on poor-quality land and food scraps, converting them into useful food energy.

Free-range pig
Cow
Lowland sheep

Medium-grade feeders, such as most Western cattle and lowland sheep, need good-quality grassland, but can also eat the remains of crops after harvesting and other plant matter.

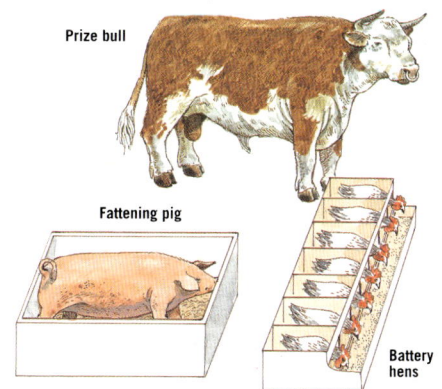
Prize bull
Fattening pig
Battery hens

High-grade feeders, such as factory-farmed cattle, pigs, and chickens, need concentrated foods, including cereal grains, that are often suitable for people to eat.

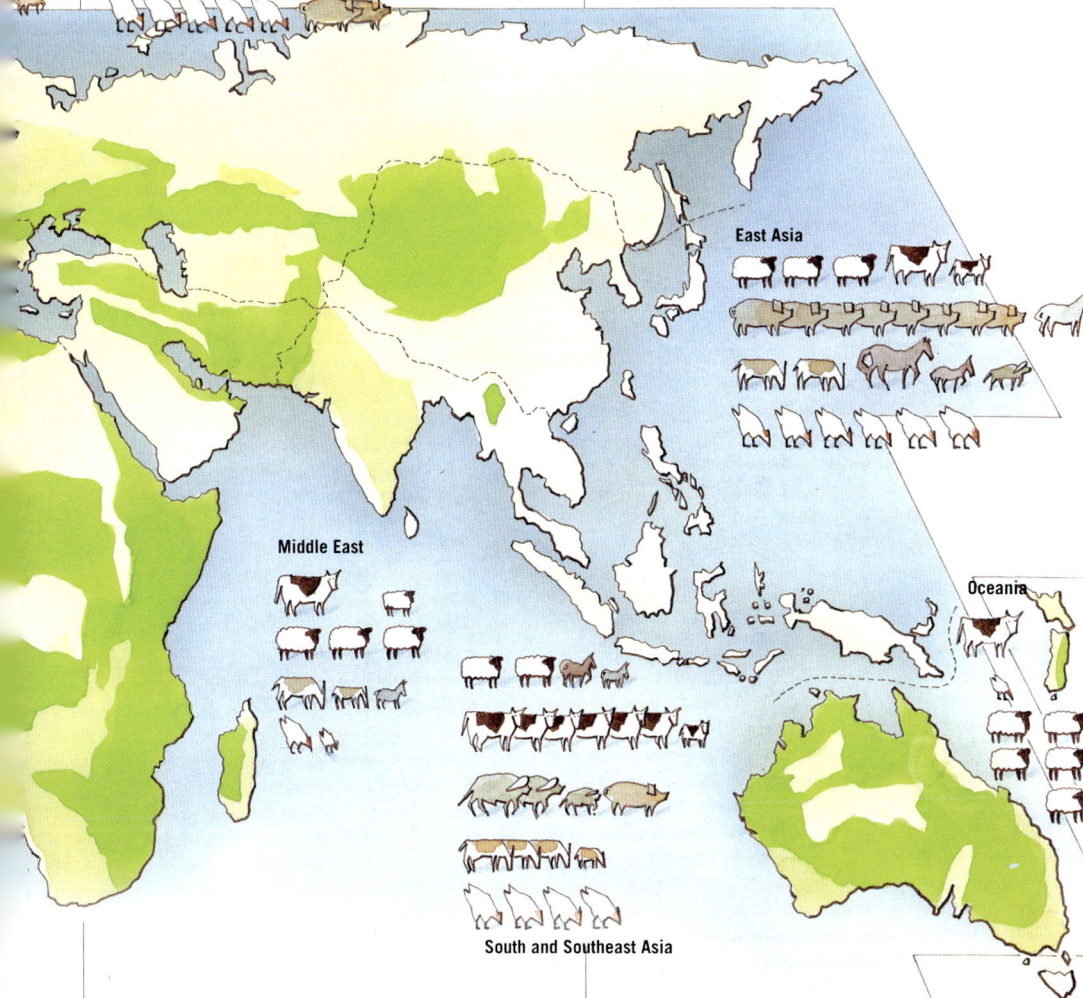
East Asia
Middle East
Oceania
South and Southeast Asia

Working animals, wool, and hides
Many of the animals that people raise have other uses besides providing food. Camels are a common method of transport in North Africa and the Middle East. Millions of farmers in developing countries use oxen (neutered male cattle) and buffalo, instead of tractors, to pull ploughs and carts. India uses 80 million animals for this form of transport.

People ride horses and use the pulling power of horses in most parts of the world, while mules and asses are used to carry loads in Central America, Africa, and East Asia. Among some African peoples, a person's position in society depends on the number of cattle that person owns. And people worldwide use non-food animal products, such as wool and hides (leather).

33

HUNGRY FOR CHANGE

Every year, 40 million people – half of them children – die from hunger and from the diseases related to it. If 300 jumbo jets crashed every day, leaving no survivors, people would be horrified – yet the number of deaths would be no greater. We seem to accept death from hunger as a fact of life.

The main cause of world hunger is not that we do not produce enough food to feed everyone. In fact, there are enough basic foods available to feed about 1500 million more people than are alive today. The problem is that not enough food reaches those who need it most. People in rich countries are supplied with too much.

They suffer the illnesses caused by overeating, and waste a lot of food. As much as a quarter of the food available to North Americans goes rotten in the supermarket or the refrigerator, or is thrown away uneaten after a meal. People in developing countries do not get enough food. Millions of children in poorer countries have a worse diet than the pet animals of people in developed countries.

More people are hungry in the world than ever before, and the numbers are growing. The situation is worst in Africa, where there is less food available for each person now than 25 years ago.

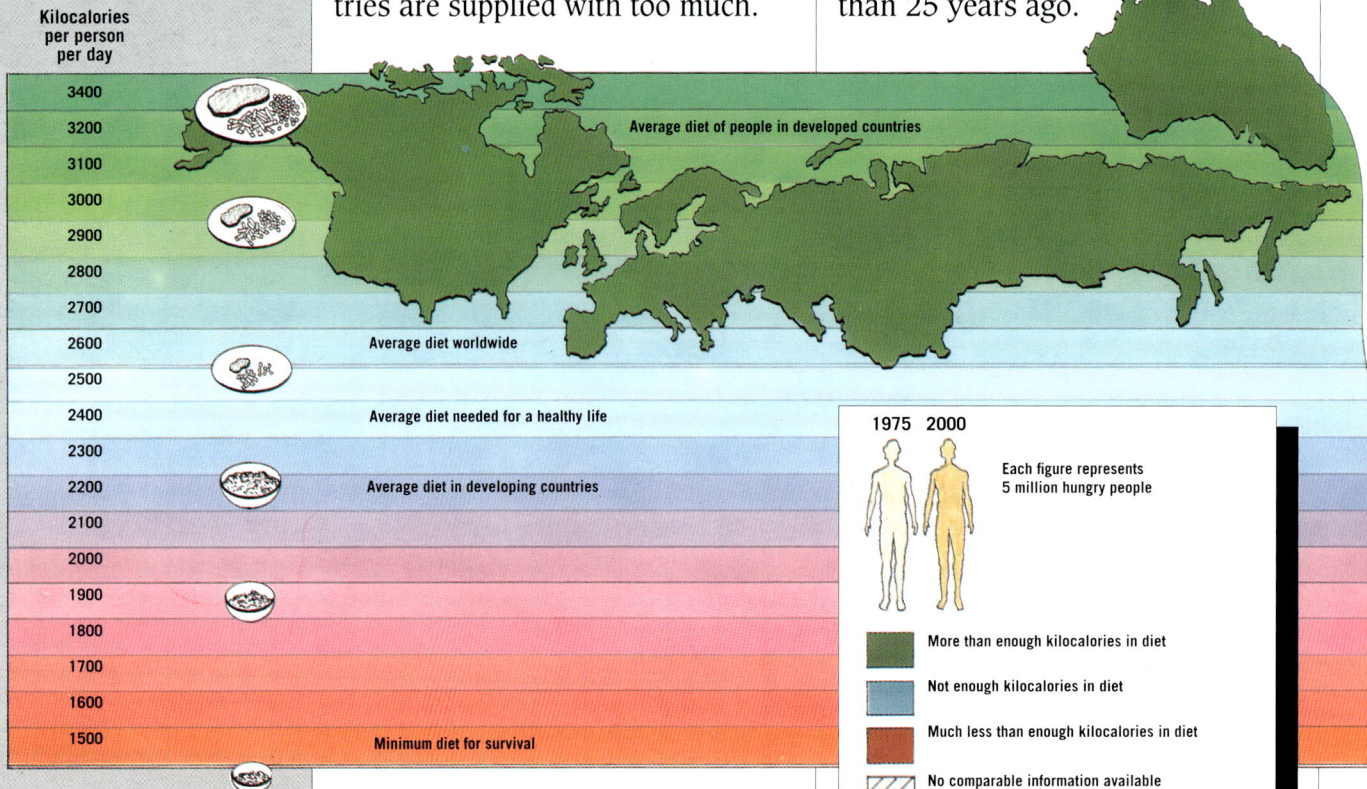

Kilocalories per person per day

3400	
3200	Average diet of people in developed countries
3100	
3000	
2900	
2800	
2700	
2600	Average diet worldwide
2500	
2400	Average diet needed for a healthy life
2300	
2200	Average diet in developing countries
2100	
2000	
1900	
1800	
1700	
1600	
1500	Minimum diet for survival

1975   2000

Each figure represents 5 million hungry people

More than enough kilocalories in diet

Not enough kilocalories in diet

Much less than enough kilocalories in diet

No comparable information available

For those of us lucky enough not to be poor, hunger lasts only as long as it takes to get to the kitchen or the food shop. But for millions of poor people around the world, hunger can mean days, months, years, or even a lifetime of suffering. All hungry people have a right to eat.

Energy for life
Each person needs an average of 2400 kilocalories (units of food energy) daily to stay healthy. Most people in developed countries have much more than this: people in developing countries usually have less than they need, so many of them die from hunger and related illnesses.

THE HUNGER GAP
Many people in the developing world receive fewer calories each day than they need, unlike most citizens of the developed world. Even more people may be undernourished by 2000.

34

Hundreds of millions of people in Asia, and many millions in Central and South America, also eat much less than they should.

Hunger causes more than physical suffering and misery. A badly nourished person cannot work properly and falls ill easily. Hungry children are unlikely to develop to their full potential.

Hunger and poverty go hand in hand. Even within developing countries rich people eat more and better food than poor people. Even so, some countries in the **South**, such as China, Sri Lanka, and Costa Rica, have managed fairer-than-average food distribution and few of their people actually starve.

The solutions do not come easily. But most concerned people agree that hunger will never be defeated without a huge effort to rid the world of poverty. Nevertheless, according to the United Nations Children's Fund, UNICEF, many of the 15 million babies and young

children who die every year in Africa, Asia, and Latin America could be saved for just $5 each. This would cover the cost of a simple sugar and salt solution to treat diarrhoea, and provide for improved **nutrition** and child health. In some places, it would also pay for extra food when it is needed. Is this too high a price for people in rich countries to pay?

Greed versus need?
Unhealthy eating habits in rich, developed countries are perhaps as much part of the world's food problems as hunger is in developing countries. Eating too much sugar, fat, salt, and animal products results in major illnesses, including obesity (the medical problem of being very overweight), heart disease, and diabetes. In countries in western Europe and North America, people spend at least four times more money on slimming aids than they do on support for hunger-relief organizations such as Oxfam, Save the Children, and Christian Aid.

HOME ACTION

We can challenge hunger and poverty by:
● eating less meat and dairy products – a field of cereals feeds 12 to 30 times more people than a field of cattle;
● eating only as much as we need to stay fit and healthy – labels on most foodstuffs provide details of daily requirements of nutrients and energy;
● buying "fair-traded" foods to help poor farmers;
● taking part in World Food Day activities, promoted by the UN Food and Agriculture Organization, on 16 October every year;
● supporting campaigning, relief, and development organizations, such as Oxfam, that work for a fairer, less hungry world.

China's war on hunger
China has been successful at sharing a limited supply of food among its people. Starvation was once common in this heavily populated country, but now it is rare. For many years the government controlled the production and distribution of food. In recent years, however, it has relaxed its control over farming and food production, allowing market forces to operate more freely. This has tended to widen the gap between rich and poor, and between well-fed and hungry.

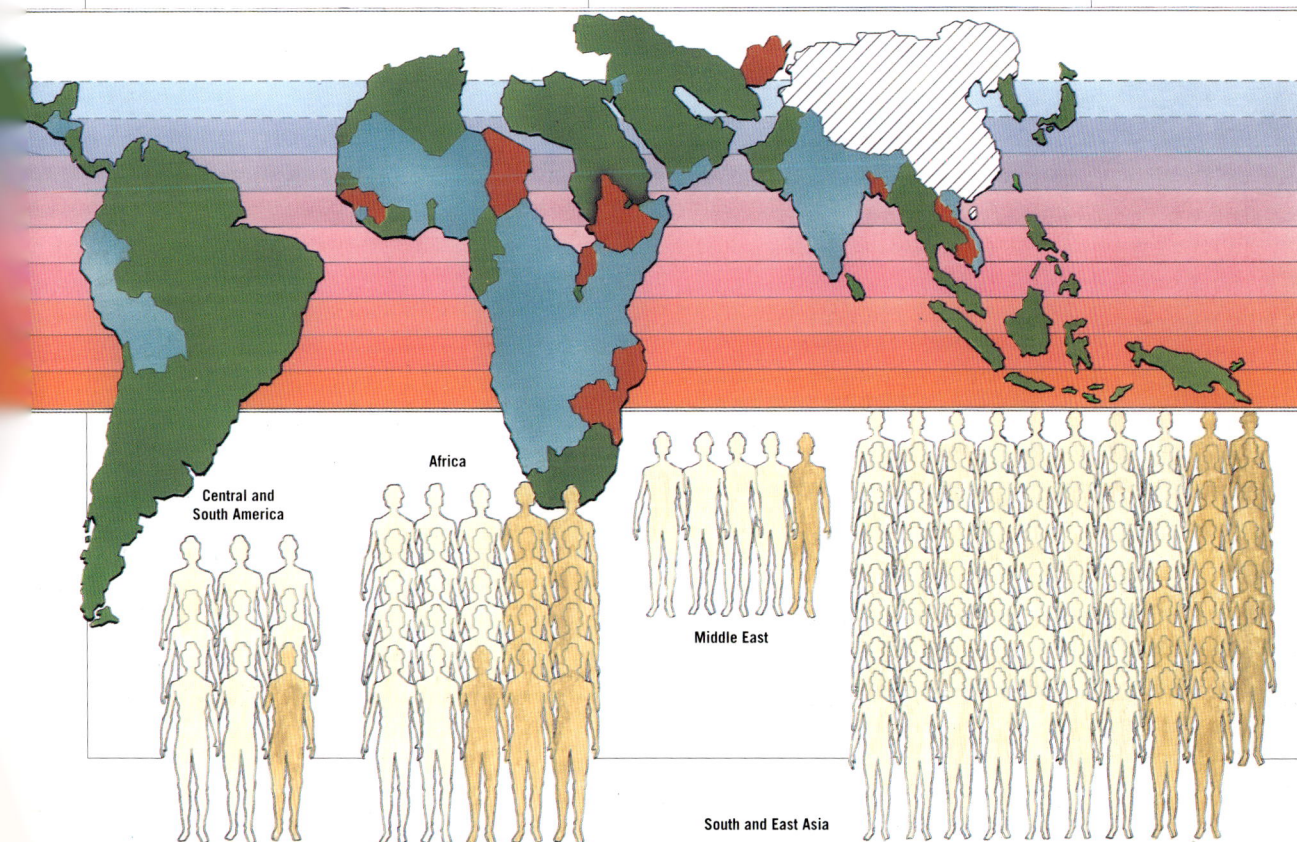

Central and South America

Africa

Middle East

South and East Asia

More and more people are going hungry. In 1975, about 435 million people worldwide had less than 1500 kilocalories a day, the very minimum needed for survival. By the year 2000, there could be 588 million severely undernourished people.

35

GLOBAL SUPERMARKET

People in developed countries can buy a huge range of foods from many lands, but their food is not always healthy or natural. Farmers who supply supermarkets with apples, for example, have to produce standard-sized fruit that will keep fresh for long periods and look good. No wonder apples are often tasteless and contain traces of the chemicals used in **pesticides** or preservatives.

Low supermarket prices have an environmental cost. Farmers may damage the countryside to produce food more cheaply and efficiently. They remove hedges and trees to enlarge fields, for example. Large quantities of fuel are used to make pesticides and to transport food and keep it fresh. Transportation also has an environmental cost. And supermarket packaging consumes enormous amounts of cardboard, paper, and plastic. Consideration of the true costs of sending food round the world might encourage local production.

Cheap food has human costs too. Low prices may be fine for large-scale farms, but small-scale farmers need fair prices. Many developing countries grow "**cash crops**" such as tea, coffee, and

Most Western farmers rely on large companies for seeds, fertilizers, and machinery, and to process their crops and sell the products. They grow as much food as they can, as quickly as possible, often helped by government grants.

A few giant companies produce and sell most of the seeds and chemicals that Western farmers use. In the USA less than 100 companies control food processing and marketing for the whole nation.

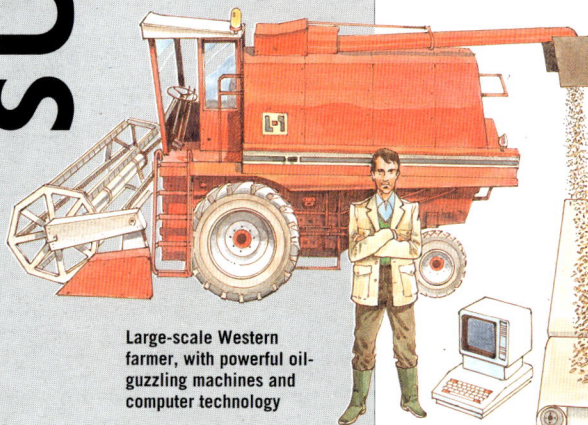

Large company, selling fertilizers and other farming chemicals, and processing and marketing food

Seeds

Pesticides

Fertilizer

GIANT

THIS

• sells

• buys

• proc

• mar

Food "inputs" (from company to farmers)

Food "outputs" (from farmers to company)

Large-scale Western farmer, with powerful oil-guzzling machines and computer technology

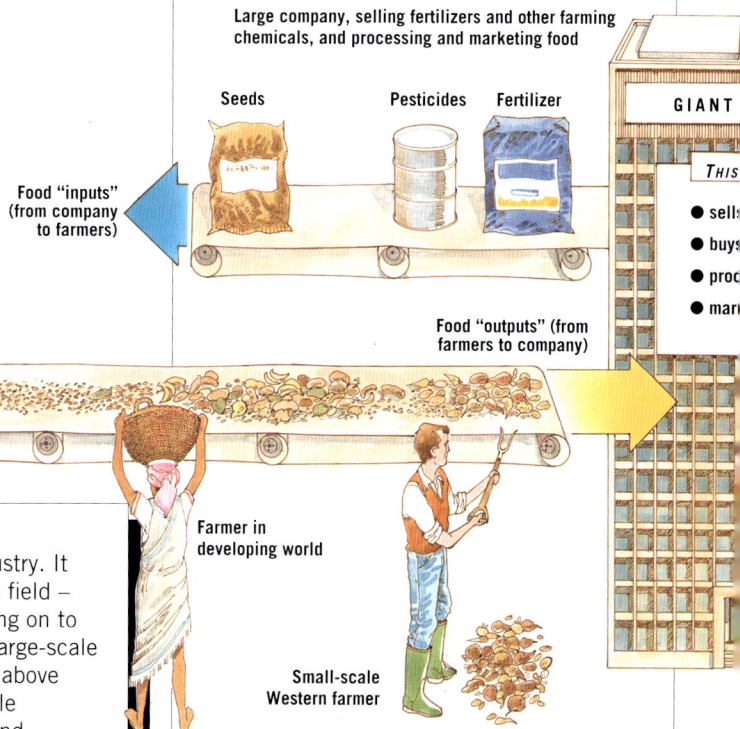

Have you ever thought about how much of your food comes from abroad? Look in your kitchen or on the supermarket shelves. The bananas are probably from the Caribbean or Latin America, the rice may be from India, the pasta from Italy, and the apples and oranges from Australia or South Africa. We enjoy eating food from all over the world, but the global supermarket has its drawbacks too.

FROM FARMER TO LARDER
Farming is a worldwide industry. It takes **raw materials** from the field – shown by the produce coming on to the conveyor belt from the large-scale Western farmer's harvester (above left) and from the small-scale developing country farmer and Western farmer (right) – and processes and packages them, via the supermarket (above right), into food for your dinner table.

Farmer in developing world

Small-scale Western farmer

Farmers in developing countries often grow **export** crops, such as coffee, instead of food that local people need. Others are too poor to buy fertilizer and machinery.

sugar for export on the best land, while their own people go hungry.

Western farmers are encouraged by government grants to produce as much food as possible, not only for the home market but also for export. The European Union, under its Common Agricultural Policy, pays more than $20,000 million each year to farmers. Some are **subsidized** (supported financially) to help maintain their livelihood. Overproduction has resulted in "lakes" of unwanted milk and "mountains" of surplus butter.

When unwanted food is sold off cheaply to developing countries, local suppliers have to lower prices below costs in order to compete. Local cattle farmers in West Africa have been badly hit by **imports** of low-cost European beef.

A small-scale farmer in Bolivia ferments cacao beans to produce fair-traded chocolate for sale in Europe.

Where the money goes when coffee is not "fair-traded"

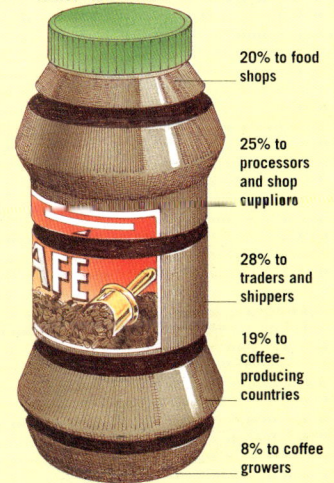

20% to food shops

25% to processors and shop suppliers

28% to traders and shippers

19% to coffee-producing countries

8% to coffee growers

Fair shares? Profits from coffee

World trade in coffee is worth thousands of millions of dollars each year. Yet only a small fraction of this money goes to the people in developing countries who grow and pick coffee beans. Huge profits are made by shippers, wholesalers, retailers, and processing companies that make dried instant-coffee powder from the beans. Today, however, "fair-trade" brands of coffee, which give local farmers a better share of the profits, are on sale in more and more shops.

Supermarket

Customers

Customer choice in supermarkets is wide, but much of this food is unhealthy and wastefully processed and packaged. People in developed countries rely more and more on convenience foods instead of having a healthy and more natural diet.

The food production line involves both small- and large-scale farmers around the world. But the developed countries benefit most from the low-cost food and cash profits.

Small-scale Western farmers do not produce as much food per worker or per hectare as large-scale farms. Many small, family farms cannot compete and go out of business.

A small number of giant companies, including financial institutions, have gained control over much of the world's food business, often working with large-scale farmers or by managing large commercial farms from a distance. Those local farmers who work on smaller areas of land find it harder to survive, although they usually farm more carefully.

Changes are needed so that everybody benefits from the global supermarket. More food should be produced locally, with less waste. Small-scale farmers and developing countries need better prices for their produce. Governments, customers, and producers need to work together to prevent damage to the environment. There are hopeful signs in our shops, such as organic (chemical-free) foods and **"fair-traded"** coffee and chocolate.

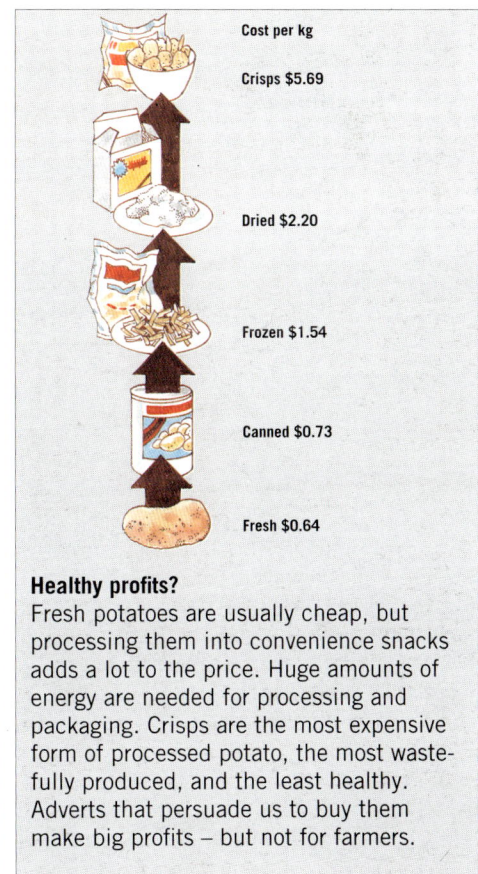

Cost per kg

Crisps $5.69

Dried $2.20

Frozen $1.54

Canned $0.73

Fresh $0.64

Healthy profits?

Fresh potatoes are usually cheap, but processing them into convenience snacks adds a lot to the price. Huge amounts of energy are needed for processing and packaging. Crisps are the most expensive form of processed potato, the most wastefully produced, and the least healthy. Adverts that persuade us to buy them make big profits – but not for farmers.

37

GREEN REVOLUTION

In the 1940s, scientists began to breed new varieties of rice, wheat, maize, and other crops. Farmers in North America and Europe who grew these new cereals using large amounts of chemical fertilizers and pesticides, and often using plenty of irrigation water, produced record grain harvests.

Soon after, farmers in Africa, Asia, and Latin America used the new seeds with similar success. In India, for example, cereal production tripled between 1950 and 1987. Throughout the world, people were able to grow more of their own food, and so relied less on costly food supplies imported from other countries.

These new **breeds** had large seed-heads and grew quickly. Many farmers found that they could harvest two or three crops a year. But success was neither certain nor never-ending. Sometimes the crops failed because farmers used too much or too little fertilizer, pesticide, or water.

World food production doubled between 1950 and 1980, largely because new cereal seeds produced bumper crops when grown in the right conditions. But these "miracle seeds" of the Green Revolution have not really solved the world's food problems.

The Muda valley project
A large, expensive river dam providing irrigation water, together with the new rice seeds of the Green Revolution, promised bigger harvests and better living standards for the people of the Muda valley in northern Malaysia. At first, farmers' harvests nearly tripled, and people were better off. But rice production stopped increasing after a few years, although more and more fertilizer was being used, because the soil had reached its natural limits. Also, fertilizer prices rose during the 1970s and farmers started to lose money. Some of them became so badly off that they sold their land in the valley to their richer neighbours, and tried to farm poor-quality forest land. The valley landscape changed as plots were combined.

Muda before the Green Revolution was a valley of small, tree-filled, family-run farms.

Muda after the Green Revolution had just a few large, treeless farms, and some families had lost their land.

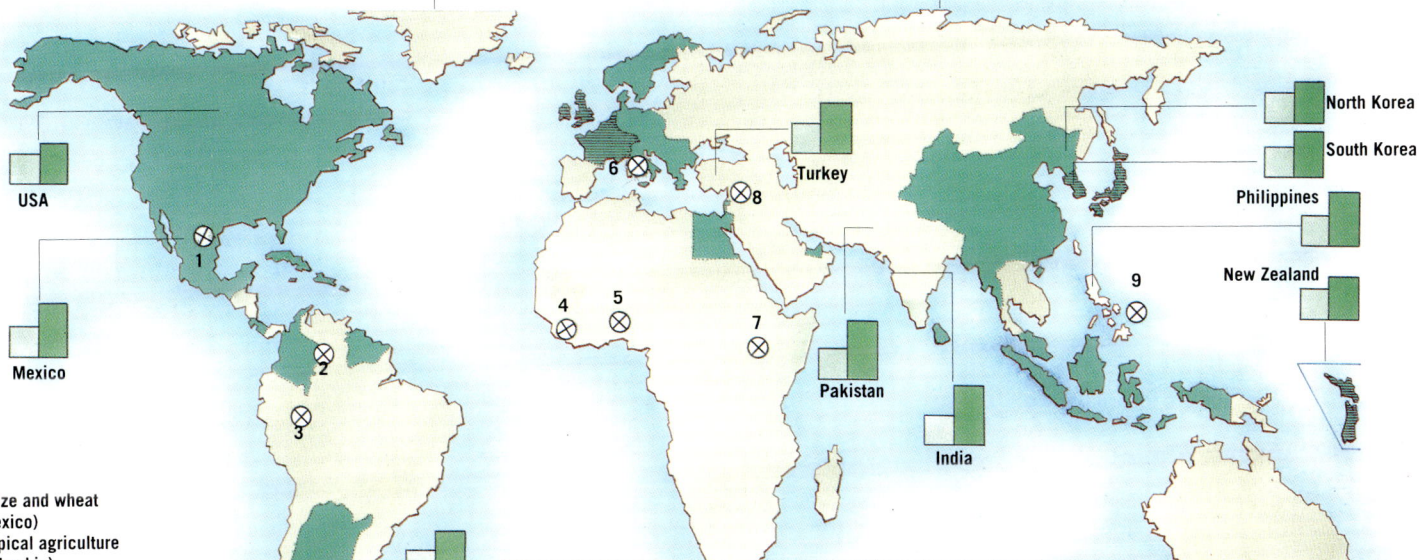

1 Maize and wheat (Mexico)
2 Tropical agriculture (Colombia)
3 Potato (Peru)
4 Rice (Liberia)
5 Tropical agriculture (Nigeria)
6 Plant breeding (Italy)
7 Animal breeding (Ethiopia)
8 Mixed farming (Lebanon)
9 Rice (Philippines)

Growth in food output 1965–81

- 1965 output
- 1981 output
- Countries with high levels of cereal production
- Countries with very high levels of cereal production
- ⊗ Main centres for agricultural research in developing countries

THE GREEN REVOLUTION
Both developed and developing countries benefited from bumper crops during the 1960s and 1970s. Since the 1980s, world food output has stopped rising. The most productive cereal lands are in western Europe, South Korea, Japan, and New Zealand.

After the revolution
Many chemical fertilizers are made from petroleum. When oil became expensive during the 1970s, many farmers could not afford to buy the fertilizers they needed. To maintain the increased harvests of the **Green Revolution**, more fertilizers and pesticides had to be used each year. Farmers found that heavy use of fertilizers and badly drained irrigation water damaged their soil.

The Green Revolution benefited some farmers more than others. The seeds, fertilizers, and other chemicals necessary were expensive, so only wealthy farmers could afford them. As they bought land from poorer neighbours with the profits of bumper harvests, the gap between rich and poor widened.

Harvests do not have to keep increasing. If we change the way we produce and distribute food, and the kind of food grown, everybody can have enough to eat.

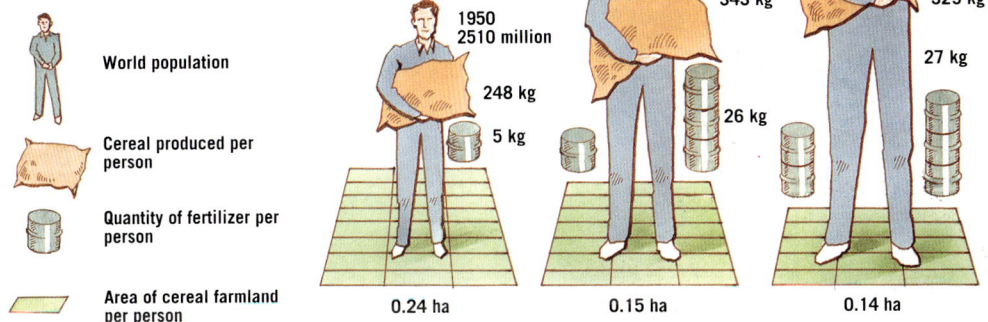

- World population
- Cereal produced per person
- Quantity of fertilizer per person
- Area of cereal farmland per person

1950 2510 million — 248 kg — 5 kg — 0.24 ha
1964 4800 million — 343 kg — 26 kg — 0.15 ha
1990s 5500 million — 329 kg — 27 kg — 0.14 ha

▲ **Between 1950 and 1990,** the world's population doubled. Farmers planted larger areas of land with cereals and used much more fertilizer to increase food production. But since 1984, they have not been able to increase food output as fast as the world population has grown, and the environment has suffered under the strain of being used ever more heavily for crop production. Less food is available in the 1990s for each woman, man, and child on the planet than there was in the mid-1960s.

HOME ACTION

Help ease the environmental problems caused by modern farming by:

- choosing local produce instead of food that has been brought long distances;
- eating fresh, rather than processed, fruit and vegetables;
- buying environment-friendly whole-foods and organic produce;
- cutting down on meat and dairy foods, so less grain is used for animal feedstuffs;
- growing your own food in a garden or on a small plot.

PASTORALISTS IN KENYA

Habiba Abdi and her family live in Wajir District in northeast Kenya. They are **pastoralists**, which means they rely on **livestock** – goats, cattle, and camels – for their livelihood. They are also **nomads**, **migrating** with their herds, following the rain in order to find good grazing land for their animals. They move on before each area is **overgrazed**. Another reason for moving on is to avoid tick-borne diseases, which spread among animals and can be passed on to people when herds are kept in one area for too long.

Habiba Abdi's day begins at dawn. The goats are milked and then taken out to graze. "We have to stay close to water with the goats and cattle, but we keep the camels away farther from the homestead so that they don't compete with the other animals for **pasture**. One of my sons looks after the camels with his family; they go wherever the rains fall.

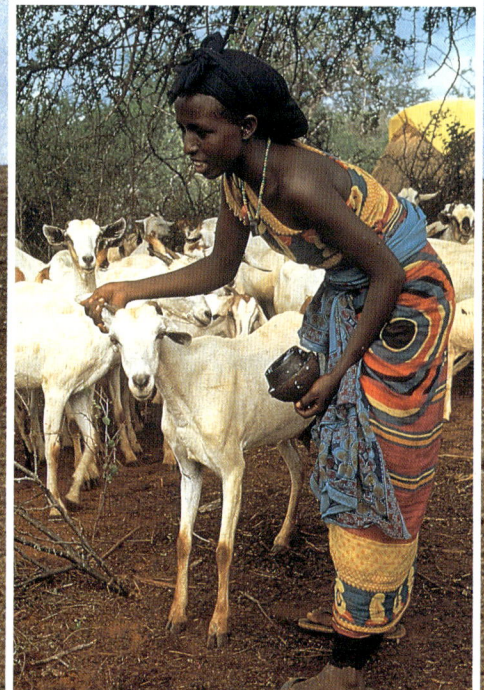

▲ **Habiba milks goats in her homestead** near Tarbaj in Wajir District. When she has finished milking each goat, its kid (young goat) is released from a pen so that it can come to suckle.

▲ **Fatima, one of Habiba Abdi's daughters,** splits palm fronds to make dufuls, the mats that are used to cover the home. Children are taught how to build houses from local plant material and how to milk goats from the age of about six. They must be able to earn their keep a few years later.

▶ **The goats are brought to a water-hole to drink,** led by Fatima. Many of the water-holes dry up within a month or two of rain falling.

There's plenty of grazing land if we just follow the rain."

Habiba lives with a group of families in a homestead. The homestead occupies an area about 80 metres in diameter, surrounded by a fence of thorn branches. Each family has one or two *herios*, houses made from branches bent to make a dome, and covered with *dufuls* – mats made from grass or palm leaves. *Herios* are quick to put up and take down, which makes it easy to move on. The thorny enclosure keeps out thieves and protects the goats from predators such as lions.

Everyone must help others when times are hard, for example during droughts. This means lending animals to friends and relatives who are not as well off. This debt may be carried on for generations but will be paid off eventually.

When Habiba's family needs money, it sells some goats, which are also exchanged for cattle and camels, instead of using money.

Pastoralism works well in areas like Wajir where there is not enough rain to grow crops. But this way of life is under threat. Many governments think pastoralists are primitive because of their ancient way of life. They like people to be settled, and to own land, not just use it. All over the world, pastoralists are under pressure to settle down and grow crops, even where the land is not good for farming.

Moving home in the Kenyan bushland (main photograph) takes no more than an hour or two, especially when everything you own – including the house, furniture, and cooking equipment – can be packed on the back of a couple of camels.

FUTURE FARMING

What kind of countryside would you like to see in 50 years' time? Wide-open treeless prairies managed by people with computers and farmed by huge oil-guzzling machines? Or a varied landscape of smaller-scale forest gardens, dotted with family households?

Farming with trees
More and more farmers are experimenting with **agroforestry** – growing trees and other crops together. Chinese farmers grow trees among wheat and tea plants. British and French farmers have planted cherry and nut trees among their cereals. The trees provide a home for small mammals and birds, helping control insect pests. In hot climates trees shade the crops, and some trees fertilize the soil with their leaves. Wood and other products from the trees help farmers earn more.

To feed the world's population adequately and protect the environment from damage, tomorrow's farming methods need to be different from today's. Many scientists, governments, and large farming businesses that produce, process, and distribute farm products favour modern, high-tech (using the latest technology) solutions. These include the **"gene revolution"** – the scientific breeding of food plants that grow well without lots of fertilizers.

Small-scale and organic farmers (who use natural methods as much as possible) prefer to combine a few new ideas with traditional, **low-tech** methods (using very little modern technology). They plant trees and hedges to encourage birds and beetles, which help to control insect pests, and in dry regions they build small rock walls to conserve water. Low-tech farming can succeed if land is shared fairly, so that all the people in a community can grow their food locally.

Better scientific research (6) will help tomorrow's farmers grow food with less harmful effects on the environment.

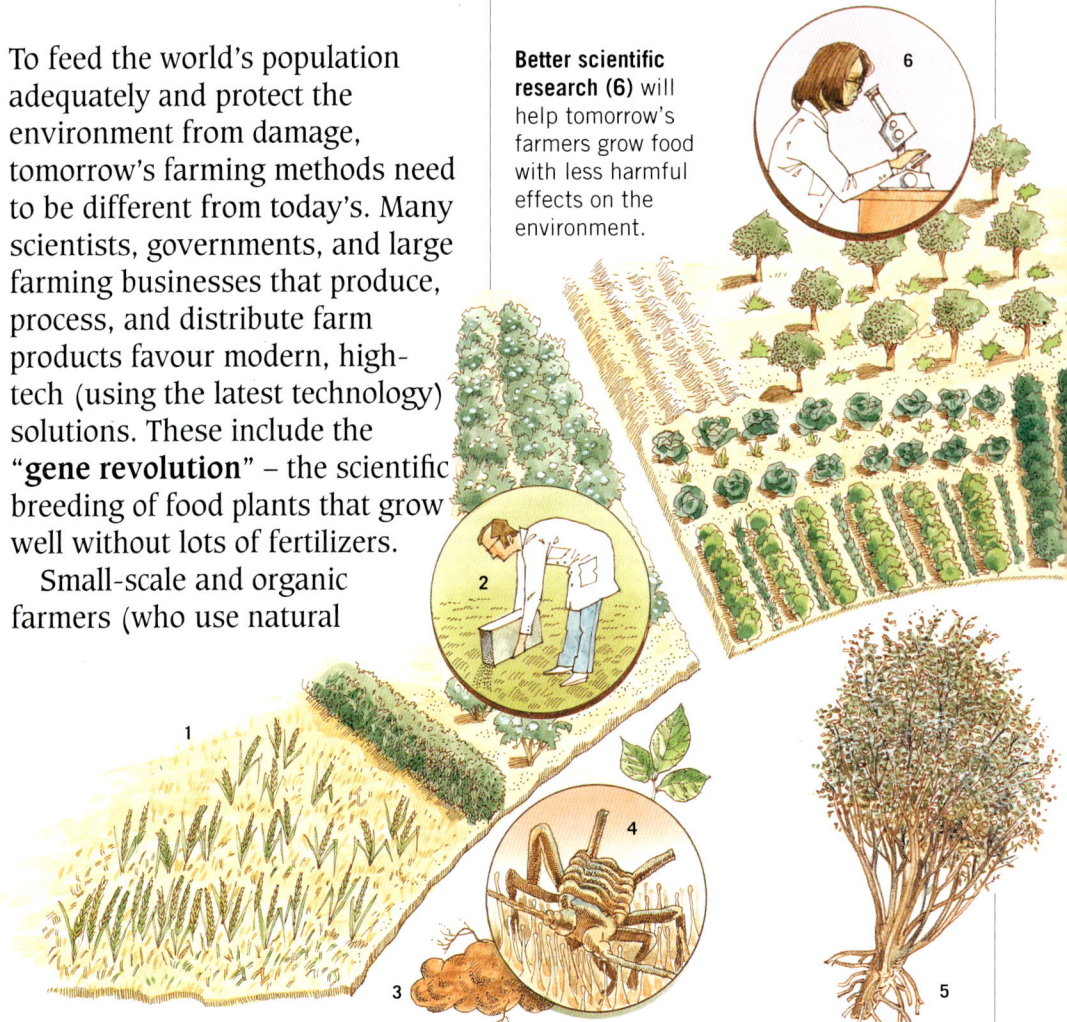

No-dig farming (1) saves energy and protects the soil. Farmers leave plant remains (called **mulches**) on the land after harvesting and do not turn over the soil before planting. **More natural pest control** reduces the farmer's reliance on chemicals **(2)**. By mixing and rotating crops, encouraging the natural enemies of pests, as well as laying bait, farmers can keep pests down.

Plants that are well adapted to harsh conditions may be useful in future. **The hairy wild potato (3)** has a natural scent that keeps away insects **(4)**. This feature could be bred into crops. **The yeheb bush (5)** has edible seeds and grows well in deserts.

This is especially important in developing countries, where small-scale farmers are the key to producing enough food. If less land is used to grow crops for export, more land can be used for food for local people. Small-scale farmers need fair market prices, loans for investment, grants to improve their farming methods, and reliable transport to local markets.

Women produce half the world's food. Their knowledge and skills

42

Mixed cropping (7) means growing different crops (including trees) together, or one after another. The choice of crops, or the order in which they are grown (**crop rotation**), is designed to conserve moisture, enrich and maintain the goodness of the soil, and keep the number of pests at a manageable level.

Different plant varieties will be stored in local **seed banks (8)**, allowing farmers to choose the most suitable types for their needs.

A BETTER KIND OF FARMING
Farming needs to change for the better. Plenty of good ideas and methods are available, many of them working towards the benefit of the environment, the farmer, and the consumer. They involve scientific research, careful land management, and the conservation of resources.

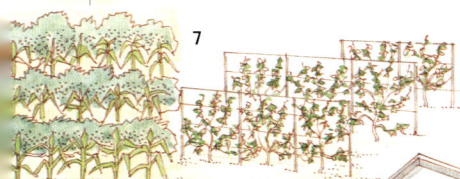
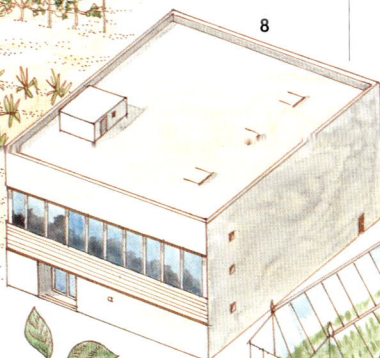
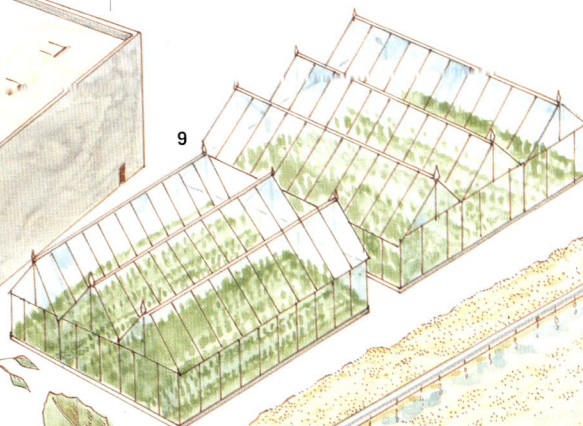

Greenhouses (9) and plastic tunnels (polytunnels) help farmers grow food on land that might otherwise not be suitable.

Trickle-drip irrigation (10) uses less water than other methods, and reduces the amount of salt left in the soil.

DID YOU KNOW?

A better way to feed the world
It takes almost 800 kg of cereals – used as feed for animals – to produce the meat that an average North American eats in a year. This is nearly five times more grain than a reasonably well-fed African eats in a year. A change in the meat-rich diet of one could help provide an adequate diet for several others.

Spirulina (11), a protein-rich algae, will grow in salt lakes in arid regions. **The winged bean (12)** was originally from the forests of New Guinea. Now farmers in 50 countries raise this nutritious crop for its high levels of protein and vitamins.

The pomelo (13) is the largest **citrus** fruit (in the same plant family as oranges and lemons). Originally from Southeast Asia, it is a good source of vitamins and food fibre, and could be a major new fruit crop in the future.

as small-scale farmers, especially in developing regions, will be important in the future.

In the developed world, more people need to adopt a less wasteful diet. By returning to the reduced-meat diets of just 30 years ago, they could improve their health and release food and land to cater for other people's needs. Soils in these regions that are over-worked today will benefit from more gentle farming methods.

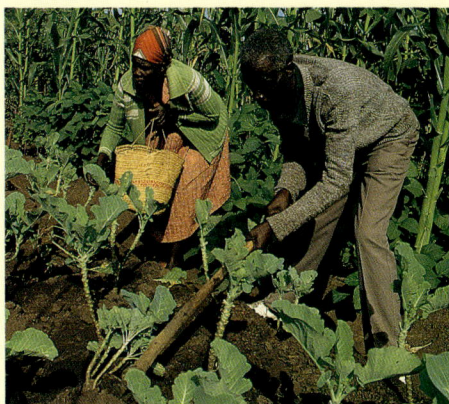

Permaculture: making the most of nature
Permaculture (short for permanent agriculture) is a labour-saving form of organic farming that combines as many different food plants, fruit and nut trees, and animals as possible. Plants are grown close together to squeeze out the weeds. Chickens and ducks are reared among the plants. Their droppings improve the soil, and they eat any weeds that do appear. Permaculture farmers collect rainwater for use in **fish farming** and grow fruit bushes as hedges. The aim of this method of farming is to feed people, avoid pollution, and save energy: it works.

WORLD MAP: POLITICAL

CONTINENTS AND REGIONS

The world's land area consists of a number of main landmasses, which we call continents. In descending order of size, the seven continents are: Asia, 43,608,000 km²; Africa, 30,335,000 km²; North and Central America, 25,349,000 km²; South America, 17,611,000 km²; Antarctica, 13,340,000 km²; Europe, 10,498,000 km²; and Australia, 7,682,300 km².

We use the names of continents and regions as if they are simple geographical facts. But definitions can vary:

The Antarctic refers to the continent of Antarctica and its surrounding seas, that is, the south polar region south of the Antarctic Circle.

The Arctic refers to the north polar ice cap and the north polar region north of the Arctic Circle.

Australasia consists of Australia, New Zealand, and the South Pacific islands. Sometimes the term Oceania is used, referring to not only Australasia but also the Central Pacific islands and the Malay islands of Southeast Asia.

The Caribbean region consists of the Caribbean Sea and its islands, but also usually Guyana on the South American coast.

Central America is the narrow strip of land connecting North America to South America – usually from the southern border of Mexico south to the northwestern border of Colombia.

Central Asia consists of the now independent Central Asian countries of the former Soviet Union, plus Mongolia, and sometimes northern China.

The East refers generally to Asia, as opposed to Europe and North America. From 1945 to 1990 the term also included the Soviet Union and communist countries of Eastern Europe.

Eastern Europe usually means all the former communist countries of Europe, to the east of what was West Germany.

The Far East refers to the countries of East Asia, including China, Japan, North and South Korea, and eastern Siberia, as well as countries in Southeast Asia, such as Malaysia.

Latin America consists of Central and South America and the Caribbean islands where most people speak Spanish or Portuguese. French-speaking Caribbean countries, such as Haiti, are sometimes included.

The Middle East (also called the Near East) is the eastern Mediterranean region, from Libya and Egypt in the west to Yemen in the south and Iran in the east.

North and **South** mean roughly "developed" and "developing". All developed countries apart from Australia and New Zealand are in the northern hemisphere; most countries in the southern hemisphere are developing ones.

North Africa consists of all African countries to the north of the Sahara Desert, notably Morocco, Algeria, Tunisia, Libya, and Egypt.

North America consists of Canada, Mexico, and the USA. Greenland, the world's largest island, is sometimes included.

Scandinavia means strictly Norway and Sweden, but more broadly can include Denmark, Finland, and Iceland.

The West means countries of the western hemisphere, seen as politically and historically different from the East. Politically, the term refers mainly to Western Europe and North America.

Western Europe generally refers to all European countries west of (and including) Germany and Austria. Greece, which belongs to the European Union, is often included.

LARGEST COUNTRIES BY SIZE AND POPULATION

Russia (officially called the Russian Federation) is the world's largest country in terms of land area; it covers 17,075,000 km², and extends from eastern Scandinavia and eastern Europe to northeast Asia. Then, in descending order, come: Canada, 9,922,385 km²; China, 9,597,000 km²; the United States of America, 9,363,130 km²; Brazil, 8,511,965 km²; Australia, 7,682,300 km²; and India, 3,166,830 km².

According to UN figures (1995), countries with the largest populations are: China, 1221 million; India, 936 million; the USA, 263 million; Indonesia, 198 million; Brazil, 169 million; Russia, 147 million; Pakistan, 140 million; Japan, 125 million; Bangladesh, 120 million; and Nigeria, 112 million. The total population of developed countries, including the former Soviet Union and Eastern Europe, was 1167 million in 1995. The total population of developing countries was 4550 million, making a world population total of 5717 million.

Norway
Sweden
Finland
Estonia
Latvia
Lithuania
Denmark
United Kingdom
Ireland
Netherlands
Belarus
Poland
Germany
Belgium
Luxembourg
Czech Republic
Slovakia
Ukraine
Liechtenstein
Austria
Hungary
Moldova
Switzerland
Slovenia
Croatia
France
San Marino
Bosnia & Herzegovina
Romania
Yugoslavia
Monaco
Bulgaria
Andorra
Italy
Macedonia
Vatican City
Albania
Portugal
Spain
Greece

Arctic Ocean
Russia
Kazakhstan
Mongolia
Georgia
Armenia
Azerbaijan
Uzbekistan
Turkmenistan
Kyrgyzstan
Tajikistan
Turkey
North Korea
South Korea
Japan
China
North Pacific Ocean
Morocco
Tunisia
Lebanon
Israel
Syria
Jordan
Iraq
Iran
Afghanistan
Kuwait
Pakistan
Nepal
Bhutan
Algeria
Libya
Egypt
Saudi Arabia
Qatar
United Arab Emirates
Bangladesh
India
Taiwan
Tropic of Cancer
Mauritania
Mali
Niger
Chad
Oman
Arabian Sea
Myanmar
Sudan
Eritrea
Yemen
Thailand
Vietnam
Philippines
Burkina Faso
Djibouti
Cambodia
Guinea
Nigeria
Benin
Togo
Ghana
Ivory Coast
Liberia
Central African Republic
Ethiopia
Sri Lanka
Cameroon
Somalia
Brunei
Malaysia
Equatorial Guinea
Uganda
Maldives
Gabon
Congo
Rwanda
Kenya
Zaire
Burundi
Seychelles
Indonesia
Equator
Tanzania
South Pacific Ocean
Papua New Guinea
Solomon Islands
Indian Ocean
South Atlantic Ocean
Angola
Zambia
Malawi
Mozambique
Vanuatu
Madagascar
Namibia
Zimbabwe
Mauritius
Botswana
Australia
Tropic of Capricorn
Swaziland
South Africa
Lesotho
New Zealand
Southern Ocean

GLOSSARY

Agroforestry A system of farming that combines trees and crops.
Atmosphere The thin layer of gases surrounding the Earth.

Bacteria Tiny, one-celled organisms.
Biomass The living weight or chemical energy contained in plants or animals.
Big Bang The supposed beginning of the universe in a single cosmic explosion about 15,000 million years ago.
Biosphere The thin layer containing all living things surrounding the Earth.
Breed A group within a plant or animal species that human management has made different from the rest of the species.

Carbohydrates Natural substances containing carbon, hydrogen, and oxygen that animals need for food: for example, sugar and starch.
Carbon dioxide A gas combining carbon and oxygen, produced by living things during respiration (e.g. through breathing), and by the rotting of organic matter and the burning of fuel.
Cash crop Farm produce grown for sale, often abroad, not for local use.
Cereal A member of the grass family of plants.
Chlorophyll The green colouring matter in plants that absorbs light energy during photosynthesis.
Citrus The family of fruits including oranges and lemons.
Climate The usual weather conditions of an area.
Coniferous Describing cone- and needle-bearing trees that are mostly evergreen.
Consumption The act of using up a resource or product.
Continent One of the Earth's large landmasses.
Coral reef A ridge in the sea formed from the skeletons of dead coral creatures.
Crop rotation The growing of different crops on the same

piece of land from one year to the next in a repeating cycle, usually four years.
Cultivate To grow plants.

Deciduous Trees and shrubs that lose all their leaves at the end of the growing season each year.
Deforestation The cutting or destruction of trees over a wide area.
Desertification The appearance of desert-like conditions in once fertile areas.
Developed country A country where large-scale industry, based on the burning of fossil fuels, is well established and usually the main source of jobs and wealth creation.
Developing country A country where farming, rather than large-scale industry, is still the main way of life.
Development Growth or progress; in economics, change whereby a community or a country becomes more effective at meeting its needs.
Domesticate To bring or keep animals or plants under control.
Drylands Areas of low rainfall.
Dyke A wall or embankment built to hold back water.

Environment The surroundings in which a plant or animal lives.
Erosion The wearing away of soil or rock by, for example, ice, rainfall, or the wind.
Evolve To develop gradually.
Evolution Gradual change in an animal or plant over several or many generations.
Export To sell to another country.

Factory farming Raising animals close together in factory-like conditions.
Fair trade A scheme to help low-income producers by buying their goods or services directly from them, rather than through agents, and at better-than-usual prices.
Fallow Farmland left unused, without crops grown on it.
Fertile Describing land or soil

that has plenty of the nutrients that plants need for growth.
Fertilizer A substance that makes the soil more fertile when added to it.
Fish farming Raising fish in captivity for food.
Fodder Food for domesticated animals.
Forestry The management of forest lands.
Fuelwood Firewood.

Gene revolution Major, rapid changes in populations of food crops and animals resulting from scientific breeding.
Global warming The probable raising of average temperatures on the Earth caused by the greenhouse effect.
Grains Cereal crops.
Greenhouse effect The trapping of the Sun's heat close to the Earth by gases in the atmosphere.
Green Revolution The change of farming methods in many developing countries since the 1940s based on the use of chemical fertilizers, pesticides, irrigation water, and specially bred crops.
Hardwoods Broad-leaved trees of hard wood.
Harvest A season's crop when ready for collection and use.
Hectare A metric measure of land area, one-hundredth of a square kilometre.
Hemisphere Half the Earth, divided north and south, or east and west.
High-tech Using modern, complicated technology.
Humus Rotted remains of plant and animal matter in soil.

Import To buy from another country.
Industry Organized activities concerned with processing raw materials to produce a wide variety of things that people use, including food.
Industrial Revolution The 18th- and 19th-century development of large-scale industrial manufacturing in the countries

of Western Europe and North America.
Irrigation The supply of water to farmland to improve crop growth.

Legume A pea- or bean-like plant or tree, bearing seeds in pods.
Livestock Animals, such as cattle, sheep, pigs, and goats, that are kept for food and other needs.
Logging Large-scale cutting of forest trees.
Low-tech Using as little complicated modern technology as possible.

Maize A cereal species grown for its edible grains.
Mangrove A tropical evergreen tree or shrub growing by the sea.
Microbe Any tiny organism that is invisible to the naked eye.
Migration Movement of people, animals, or plants from one place to settle in another. In birds and other animals this often occurs in a seasonal cycle.
Mineral Any solid, non-plant and non-animal, naturally occurring material.
Mulch A layer of half-rotted plant remains to protect the soil.

Nomad A person who travels with domesticated animals in search of pasture for them.
North The developed countries of Western Europe, North America, Japan, and Australasia.
Nutrients Substances that plants need for growth.
Nutrition Nourishment with food.

Organic Living.
Organic farming Farming without the use of human-made chemicals, relying on natural methods.
Organism A living animal or plant.
Overfarming The cultivation of crops to the extent that the fertility of the soil is reduced or completely destroyed.
Overfishing Taking more fish from the seas than the natural reproduction can replace.

Overgrazing Vegetation damage caused by domesticated animals stripping the land of plant matter.

Pastoralist A person who raises livestock for a living.
Pasture Land covered by grass or other vegetation suitable for grazing livestock.
Percent(age) Out of every 100.
Permaculture Organic farming based on growing together as many plant and animal species as possible.
Permafrost Permanently frozen ground in high-latitude regions that does not thaw even in summer and has been frozen for years.
Pesticide A chemical used to kill animal or plant pests.
Photosynthesis The process by which plants use the Sun's energy to make their own food from carbon dioxide and water, releasing oxygen as a by-product of the process.
Pollution Any substance that interferes with and harms natural processes when added to the natural environment.
Polytunnel A polythene tunnel used for crop growing.
Protein Any one of a large group of chemical compounds that all living things have within them.
Pulse A plant in the pea and bean family.

Rainforest Species-rich forest in areas of heavy rainfall.
Raw material A naturally occurring substance used to make something else.
Recycling Using or processing materials (or energy) more than once.
Resistance In farming, the ability of a crop or a group of domesticated animals to withstand a pest or disease.
Resource A natural material or process (such as water flow) that provides energy or materials.

Seed bank A store of plant seed varieties.
South The developing countries of Africa, Asia, the Caribbean, Central and South America, and the Pacific.
Species A complete group of living organisms that can breed together and produce offspring.
Subsidize To give financial help.

Terrace A flat area of land, often part of a series of flat "steps" constructed to allow farming on steep hillsides.
Topsoil The layer of soil nearest the land surface.
Tropics The high-temperature regions of the Earth's surface to the north and south of the equator.
Tundra Cold, treeless lands between the polar ice cap and northernmost forests.

Ultraviolet An invisible form of light that can tan and burn exposed human skin.
UV Ultraviolet.

Vapour A mass of small droplets of a liquid in the air.
Vegetation Living plants.

Wetlands Flood plains, mangroves, marshes, swamps, and mud-flats close to a river, a lake, or the sea.

Yield The amount or quality of a crop.

INDEX

Headwords refer to information in texts or captions but not maps. **Bold** page numbers refer to main entries in text.